Part of Nature

Also by Genevieve Lloyd

The Man of Reason: "Male" and "Female" in Western Philosophy

Being in Time: Selves and Narrators in Philosophy and Literature

Part of Nature

Self-Knowledge in Spinoza's *Ethics*

Genevieve Lloyd

Cornell University Press
Ithaca and London

A section of Chapter 1 first appeared in different form in Genevieve Lloyd, "Spinoza's Version of the Eternity of the Mind," in *Spinoza and the Sciences,* edited by Marjorie Grene and Debra Nails, pp. 211–36 (Boston Studies in the Philosophy of Science, vol. 91) (Dordrecht: Reidel, 1986). Reprinted by permission of Kluwer Academic Publishers. An earlier version of a section of Chapter 2 first appeared in Genevieve Lloyd, "Spinoza on the Distinction between Intellect and Will," in *Spinoza: Issues and Directions,* edited by Edwin Curley and Pierre-François Moreau (Leiden: E. J. Brill, 1990).

First published 1994 by Cornell University Press.

Library of Congress Cataloging-in-Publication Data

Lloyd, Genevieve.
    Part of nature : self-knowledge in Spinoza's Ethics / Genevieve Lloyd.
       p. cm.
    Includes bibliographical references and index.
    ISBN 0-8014-2999-4 (alk. paper)
    1. Spinoza, Benedictus de, 1632–1677. Ethica. 2. Self-knowledge, Theory of. 3. Self (Philosophy) 4. Ethics. I. Title.
B3974.L56 1994
170-dc20   94-3194

For Amélie Oksenberg Rorty

O

Contents

Abbreviations

Works

AT   Charles Adam and Paul Tannery, eds. *Oeuvres de Descartes.* 11 vols. Paris: Vrin, 1974–86.

C.   Edwin Curley, ed. *The Collected Works of Spinoza.* Princeton: Princeton University Press, 1985.

Cott.   John Cottingham, Robert Stoothoff, and Dugald Murdoch, eds. *The Philosophical Writings of Descartes.* 2 vols. Cambridge: Cambridge University Press, 1985.

G.   Carl Gebhardt, ed. *Spinoza Opera.* 4 vols. Heidelberg: Carl Winter, 1925.

References to Spinoza's *Ethics*

A	Axiom
App	Appendix
C	Corollary
Def	Definition
Def. Aff.	Definitions of the Affects
Dem	Demonstration
Exp	Explanation
Gen. Def. Aff.	General Definition of the Affects
P	Proposition
Pref	Preface
S	Scholium
sect.	Section

O

Introduction

The idea of human beings as part of nature has diverse—and often conflicting—associations. It resonates in contemporary consciousness with the history of Romanticism, evoking nostalgic yearnings for uncorrupted experience and for lost unities of passion and reason, for an undivided human nature responding spontaneously to a world with which it forms a whole. Contemporary aspirations to an undivided unity with nature link us, through the Romantics, to Rousseau's dream of reattaining a closeness to nature through a transformed version of reason—reflective without abstraction, lively and imaginative without loss of judgment. It is a vision largely formed in reaction against the heritage of seventeenth-century rationalist philosophy. But also implicit in the idea of ourselves as part of nature is another strand, which belongs with those older rationalist ideals to which Romanticism is, perhaps all too readily, seen as diametrically opposed: a commitment to the idea that human beings, no less than the rest of reality, can be understood through rational, scientific method.

In exploring the connections between these two threads—apparently so different—of the idea that we are part of nature, the study of Spinoza is crucial. His thought occupies a strangely ambiguous position. It belongs, on the one hand, firmly with the rationalist tradition—with the philosophies of Descartes and Leibniz. He extols the rationalist ideal of the world as an ordered, intelligible whole, subject neither to the intrusions of divine purpose nor to the vagaries of an erratic human will. Yet his thought also has clear affinities with later attitudes associated with Romanticism. Although Spinozism is seriously at odds with assumptions of seventeenth-century rationalism, it is also their logical outcome—a view of human beings and their relation to the rest of nature which is both continuous with and radically different from the Cartesian philosophy from which it sprang.

Edwin Curley, in his excellent discussion of the relations between Descartes's and Spinoza's metaphysics in *Behind the Geometrical Method*,[1] suggests that tracing the steps by which Spinoza derived the central themes of the *Ethics* from critical reflection on the Cartesian system might make Spinoza's philosophy more accessible, less esoteric, than it often seems to contemporary readers. When Descartes published his *Meditations*, Curley observes, it was a revolutionary work. But in the three and a half centuries that have passed since then, its ideas have seeped sufficiently into consciousness to have become part of "educated common sense," much as Aristotle's philosophy had when Descartes wrote. So to derive Spinoza's thought from Descartes's can be seen as a way of trying to make its abstractions seem intelligible and reasonable—a way of going from the relatively familiar and natural to the unfamiliar and, prima facie, implausible. Curley is undoubtedly right in suggesting that some of the most distinctive features of Spinoza's philosophy arose from internal tensions within the Cartesian system. However, in this book I pursue the connections between Descartes and Spinoza from the other direction. Rather than seeing those connections as making Spinoza clearer to "educated common sense," I want to explore the ways in which Spinoza's exposure of the ambivalences in Descartes's philosophy illuminates the strangeness of our own commonsense assumptions about our position in the world—about individuality and selfhood.

The individuality of the Cartesian self gives way in Spinoza's phi-

1. Edwin Curley, *Behind the Geometrical Method* (Princeton: Princeton University Press, 1988), p. 3.

losophy, as we shall see, to a way of thinking of the self as part of an interconnected totality—as itself, in a new way, part of nature. For Descartes the mind could be said to be part of nature in the sense that, like the rest of creation, it depended on God. But its status as individual intellectual substance set it apart from other things. As a self-contained unity, the Cartesian mind forms part of a whole with neither God nor world. Even the unity it forms with its own body is strangely tenuous. For Descartes, the human body's status as part of nature marked an expansion of the scope of science. As bodies, we are no less accessible to scientific understanding than is the rest of nature. But his model of knowledge left the mind separate from the rest of nature in ways that opened space also for later Romantic yearnings for a supposedly lost unity. As minds we remain separate from the rest of the world—self-contained intellectual substances, knowable through an introspection that, however, leaves us strangely lacking in individuality. In knowing himself, as he assures his readers in the *Meditations,* Descartes finds nothing that is not equally available to all who reflectively follow his method for reaching certainty. Cartesian selves are ambiguously located between the individuality of substancehood and the universality of reason. Spinozistic selves rejoin nature through the individuality of bodies construed as uniquely differentiated parts of nature. Spinoza takes seriously the inclusion of minds, no less than bodies, in the totality of nature. The result, far from being an abandonment of selfhood, is an innovative treatment of individuality that brings together metaphysics and ethics.

Gilles Deleuze has commented on the unusual ways in which Spinoza's philosophy combines a highly developed systematic and scholarly approach to philosophy with an immediacy that can impart a "sudden illumination" to non-philosophers.[2] Although he is one of the most difficult and demanding of philosophers, he offers, more

2. Gilles Deleuze, *Spinoza: Practical Philosophy,* trans. Robert Hurley (San Francisco: City Lights Books, 1988), p. 129.

than most philosophers, a wealth of insights, a source of wisdom for practical living. This book attempts to make accessible the connections between metaphysics and ethics that center on his distinctive account of individuality without substancehood. It explores the ethical implications of Spinozistic self-knowledge and their timeliness in relation to some of the most morally perplexing aspects of contemporary self-consciousness.

ONE

O

Substance and Selfhood

Spinoza has become notorious for his doctrine of the uniqueness of substance. For him there is but one self-contained being. Matter and mind alike are attributes of it, and finite material and mental things are modifications of it. Spinoza's contemporaries regarded the doctrine as perverse and pernicious. An entry on Spinoza in Bayle's *Dictionary* described it as having implications that surpassed the fantastic ravings of the maddest heads that were ever locked up.[1] Bayle was outraged by the theological and moral implications of Spinoza's philosophy. If all things are modes of the one substance, the atrocities that human beings inflict on one another cease to be the responsibility of individuals and become the self-mutilations of an all-encompassing God. By the time Hegel articulated his misgivings about Spinoza's substance, he was able to draw on much more fully developed ideals of autonomous individual selfhood. But the basic fear was the same—the engulfing of selfhood and autonomy in the oneness of things.

Hegel's attitude to Spinoza's substance was ambivalent. In his *Lectures on the History of Philosophy*[2] he expressed both repugnance for

1. Pierre Bayle, Entry on "Spinoza" from *Dictionnaire, historique et critique* in *Ecrits sur Spinoza: Textes choisis et présentés par Françoise Charles-Daubert et Pierre-François Moreau* (Paris: Berg International Editeurs, 1983), pp. 23, 68–70.
2. Quotations are from Hegel, *Lectures on the History of Philosophy* (1896), trans. Elizabeth S. Haldane and Frances H. Simson (London: Routledge and Kegan Paul; New York: Humanities Press, 1974), vol. 3, pp. 252–90.

Spinoza's apparent rejection of individuality and attraction for the "grandeur" which allowed him to renounce all that is determinate and particular, restricting himself to the One. To bathe, like Spinoza, in the "ether of the One Substance" is, Hegel said, the essential starting point of all philosophical thought. The negation of all that is particular, to which every philosopher must have come, is the "liberation of the mind and its absolute foundation." For Spinoza, to Hegel's admiration, this philosophical commitment was total, permeating his life and even his death. His lens grinding reflects the symbolism of light as the material version of absolute identity; and the consumption from which he died was in harmony with his system, in which all particularity and individuality pass away in the one substance. For Hegel, however, the costs of this metaphorical consumption were unacceptably high. Spinoza casts self and world into the abyss of the one identity, so that what *is* is "God, and God alone." The allegations of those who accuse Spinoza of atheism, Hegel suggests, are the direct opposite of the truth. With Spinoza there is "too much God." Spinoza is not up to the challenge of apprehending oneness without letting difference slip; and the result is that his substance is a static and undifferentiated reality—"the One into which everything enters, in order to be absorbed therein, but out of which nothing comes." Without individuality, there is no life or self-consciousness either. Spinoza offers us the ocean, from which self-consciousness is born—dripping with its water, but never coming to absolute selfhood.

The view of Spinoza to which Hegel gave such eloquent expression is still common, and it is not surprising that it should have prevailed so long. According to Roger Scruton, for example, Spinoza's monism denies to human persons—and indeed to everything—the status of an individual.[3] The treatment of "all that we know as the world," in Hegel's phrase, as modes of the one substance, seems to leave little room for individual existence. As mere modes within the totality of

3. Roger Scruton, *Spinoza* (Oxford: Oxford University Press, 1986), p. 53.

(6)

thought, our minds would appear to have little scope for autonomous selfhood. If particular things are indeed nothing but "affections of God's attributes, or modes by which God's attributes are expressed in a certain and determinate way" (*Ethics* IP25C), we may well seem to have lost both world and self.

Individuality does indeed have a paradoxical character in Spinoza's philosophy. Hegel's reading of him—as the philosopher of the abyss—is not fanciful. But his philosophy can also be read as a profound articulation of individuality, selfhood, and freedom. The possibility of such a reading, it is true, owes much to the ways in which Hegel developed the insights he found in Spinoza. As Pierre Macherey has commented, Hegel stands between Spinoza and ourselves, and we cannot read Spinoza today without thinking of Hegel.[4] To see in Spinoza's texts an innovative philosophy of individuality is to see him through Hegelian lenses. But that need not mean that what is distinctive in his thought is consumed in the Hegelian abyss. What is distinctive in Spinoza's version of individuality and selfhood can best be seen in the context of Descartes's philosophy, which was its starting point. If Hegel bathed in the ether of Spinoza, Spinoza bathed in the Cartesian ether; and there is irony in the fact that Spinoza was able to develop doctrines his contemporaries found pernicious from apparently innocuous beginnings in Descartes's philosophy. Spinoza presents his notorious doctrine of the uniqueness of substance as a natural development of concepts that were familiar and uncontroversial to his contemporaries—concepts of substance, attribute, and mode, drawn from the Aristotelian tradition and adapted in novel, but apparently unthreatening, ways by Descartes.

In his *Principles* Descartes defined substance as meaning a thing that exists in such a way as to depend on no other thing for its existence, and remarked that there was only one thing, namely God, which could be thus understood as dependent on nothing (Part 1, sec.

4. Pierre Macherey, *Hegel ou Spinoza* (Paris: François Maspéro, 1979), p. 9.

51; AT viiiA, 24; Cott. i, 210). All other 'substances' we perceive to exist only with the help of God's concurrence. It might seem that Descartes was himself committed to the doctrine of the uniqueness of substance. But he goes on to say that the term does not apply "*univocally,* as they say in the schools," to God and to other things. There is no distinctly intelligible meaning of the term that is common to God and his creatures. A substance, in the sense that applies to created things, is a thing that needs only the ordinary concurrence of God in order to exist. The contrast is with qualities and attributes whose dependence on other things extends beyond that ordinary concurrence of God. Mind and matter are Cartesian substances only in the secondary sense—needing nothing other than God in order to exist. We become aware of them through their attributes, principal among which are—for corporeal substance—extension and—for mind—thought. Modes are affections or modifications of substance, and qualities are a special case of modes, enabling the substance to be designated as of such and such a kind. Since God is not subject to variation, substance, in Descartes's strict sense, has neither modes nor qualities but only attributes. Even in the case of created things, he adds, that which always remains unmodified—for example, existence or duration in a thing that exists and endures—should be called not a quality or mode but an attribute (*Principles,* Part i, sect. 56; AT viiiA, 26; Cott. i, 211–12).

The individual mind is for Descartes a substance in this derivative sense. It is a self-contained, complete thing, dependent for existence on nothing outside itself, save God alone. But the individual body, he points out in the synopsis of the *Meditations* (AT vii, 14; Cott. ii, 10), does not have that status. Whereas the human body, insofar as it differs from other bodies, is simply made up of a certain configuration of limbs and "other accidents of this sort," the human mind is a pure substance, not made of accidents. Even if all the supposed accidents of the mind change, so that it has different objects of understanding and different desires and sensations, it does not on that account become a

(8)

different mind. A human body, in contrast, loses its identity merely as a result of a change in the shape of some of its parts. It follows, Descartes thinks, that while the body can very easily perish, the nature of the mind allows it to be immortal.

In Part One of the *Ethics* Spinoza realigns these concepts of substance, attribute, and mode. God becomes categorically the one and only substance. And whereas thought and extension had been for Descartes attributes of two different kinds of substance, each dependent on God, they become for Spinoza attributes of God himself. Echoing Descartes's talk of the attributes as ways in which substances come to be apprehended, Spinoza presents them as ways in which we can understand the one substance—the only two of God's infinitely many attributes of which we can be aware. All particular things, whether material or mental, become modifications of God or Substance, either under the attribute of thought or under the attribute of extension. Individual minds, no less than bodies, are modes of substance. The mind loses its status of substance, which had been so crucial for Descartes, and becomes a mere mode of God.

For Spinoza the existence of God involves the uniqueness of substance.[5] From our own perspective, his argumentation may be less than persuasive. But the assumptions that are problematic for us are not ones to which a Cartesian could readily have taken exception. Spinoza relies on the rationalist idea of causality as a relation of containment between concepts. One substance cannot produce another; for effects are conceived through their causes, and substance must be conceived through itself alone (1P6 and C). And he relies on the traditional theological claim that the most perfect being must possess all attributes. It is a pattern that recurs throughout the *Ethics,* and often the ironic intent seems very close to the surface. Spinoza

5. Edwin Curley offers an excellent account of Spinoza's argument for the uniqueness of substance, in relation to Cartesian assumptions, in chapter 1 of *Behind the Geometrical Method: A Reading of Spinoza's "Ethics"* (Princeton: Princeton University Press), 1988.

takes a Cartesian position and derives from it—by what seems a strict application of the geometrical procedure that Descartes extolled—an apparently outrageous conclusion. Here the categories of substance, attribute, and mode retain many of their Cartesian connotations. But their application has dramatically shifted. Descartes's idea of a self-completeness, independent of all external causes, remains. But that ideal now bears on human life in a very different way.

For Descartes the individual mind exemplifies the unalienable status of self-conscious autonomous substance, dependent on nothing but God. This metaphysical status gives rise to a moral ideal: we should aspire to reflect in our lives this substancehood, in which we resemble God. The Cartesian mind rightly prides itself on its god-like self-completeness. For Spinoza we are not individual substances, either as bodies or as minds. But we are nonetheless individuals. In withdrawing the status of substance from the human mind, Spinoza does not deny its individuality. And the concept of substance continues to have moral significance for human life, though in a very different way. Spinoza calls into question the traditional links between individuality and the concept of substance. And it cannot be denied that this gives his treatment of individuality a paradoxical character. But he certainly does not present individuality as an illusion. There is a false, distorted way in which a mind can think of itself and of other things as individuals—a source of error that must be transcended by a mind pursuing freedom and virtue. But in that pursuit the mind comes to a true understanding of its own individuality.

The Individuality of Bodies

It is a commonplace that Spinoza's treatment of bodies emphasizes interconnections, the importance of grasping things as parts of wholes. But it is easy to overlook just how radical is his version of that idea. It goes beyond the claim that individual bodies exist in wider environments on which they depend for their continued existence and well-being. What is novel about Spinoza's version of the theme of interconnection is that for him those wider systems—encompassing what we think of as individual bodies—are themselves individuals, in the same sense as the bodies themselves. To be a Spinozistic individual body is precisely to be part of wider wholes. It is being thus inserted into a totality that constitutes a thing's individuality.

What it is to be bodily, and what it is to be a body, are questions that receive different answers in the *Ethics;* and both are cryptic. The digression on the nature of bodies, between Propositions 13 and 14 of Part Two, is very compressed. The simplest bodies, he says there, are distinguished from one another by differences in motion and rest, and they determine one another in motion and rest to infinity. But the differences between individual bodies are determined at another level. Questions about individuality arise only at the level of composite bodies. Spinoza is not very informative about the exact nature of the singular bodies that compose them. They do not figure in the account of bodies as independent entities, but only in combination with one another. The most basic individuals are themselves composites of those simpler "singular" bodies. And it is in his treatment of these combinations that Spinoza elaborates his understanding of individuality, which is superimposed on the constant changes in motion and rest among the simplest bodies.

A thing's individuality is constituted by what Spinoza describes as the union of bodies composing it. He explains this in terms of the preservation of a certain ratio of motion and rest among its component parts, despite the constant changes among the simplest bodies involved in it. Individuals of the most basic kind involve a union of simple bodies—a union that exists as long as the ratio of motion to rest among those simple bodies is preserved, even if the bodies themselves are replaced. These first-level individuals enter into further unions of bodies, in which ratios of motion to rest are maintained, despite bodily change. A hierarchy of individuals, thus conceived, reaches up to the universe as a whole, which can itself be conceived as an individual, continuing to exist despite the generation, change, and decay that occur within it. Each individual is thus enmeshed in a more comprehensive one, reaching up to the all-encompassing individual—"the whole of nature." This insertion of individuals into ever wider ones may seem bizarre if we think of it in terms of the more traditional connections between the unity of an individual and the unity of substance. But Spinoza's hierarchy of individuals does not involve thinking of human bodies as constituents of larger organisms, or of the universe as itself an immense organism. There is no ready parallel in our own thought for what is involved in his nested embeddings of individuals. But it is nearer our modern concept of an ecosystem—an interconnected totality of organisms and their environment—than to any idea of the world as a unified body.

Spinoza elaborates on the relations between parts and wholes in an often-quoted letter to Oldenburg. A worm living in the bloodstream, he remarks there, would be able to distinguish particles within the blood and to observe their impact on one another. But it could not from its perspective grasp how these parts are controlled by the nature of the blood and are forced by it to adapt so as to harmonize with one another. Nor could it apprehend the blood as subject to external causes. Such a worm would live in the blood as we live in our part of the universe, considering each particle as a whole and not a part. All the bodies of nature, Spinoza thinks, should be conceived as he here conceives the blood, for they are all determined to exist and to act in determinate ways, while there is preserved in the whole universe the same ratio of motion and rest (G. IV, Epistola XXXII, 171–72).[6] Considered in themselves, the particles appear as independent individuals. They are not adjusted to one another. But these apparent wholes are in fact parts, having reciprocal agreements with things external to themselves. In this way, all individuals can be seen as in perpetual reciproc-

6. Translated by R. M. H. Elwes in *The Chief Works of Benedict de Spinoza* (New York: Dover, 1955), vol. 2, p. 291.

ity with one another—parts of an immense whole, the universe. Only at this point do we reach something that is not part of a wider system— something whose characteristic ratio of motion to rest is not vulnerable to the impingement of outside forces.

To see the full picture, we must take these remarks in conjunction with Spinoza's treatment, in Part Three, of the concept of *conatus*— the "striving by which each thing endeavours to persist in being." Spinoza identifies this *conatus* with the thing's "actual essence" (iiiP7). The concept is drawn from Hobbes and figures also in Leibniz's treatment of bodies. In his early work *The Theory of Abstract Motion,*[7] Leibniz argued that it is in terms of such a concept that the true distinction between mind and matter is to be understood. Every body is a momentary mind, or one lacking recollection. For it does not retain its own *conatus* and another contrary one together for longer than a moment. Body lacks memory. It lacks the perception of its actions and passions; it lacks thought. Bodies are, as it were, momentary minds, with no extension through time. In the Leibnizian version of *conatus,* mind and matter—kept so firmly apart by Descartes—draw together. Here the element of striving in matter seems to be construed quite literally. The theme persists, though less dramatically, into the *Discourse on Metaphysics,* where Leibniz argues that an adequate account of matter and motion demands the reintroduction of some aspects of the scholastic notion of "substantial forms"—those soul-like principles which Descartes, in the name of dualism, had so ruthlessly exorcised from physics (chapters 10–11). Although matter can be construed mechanistically, it cannot be fully understood without resort to final causes. Explanations in terms of efficient causality are not false. But this network of efficient causes has superimposed on it a realm of final causality that expresses its true nature. The scholastics were mistaken, Leibniz thinks, in appealing to final causes in particu-

7. Leibniz, *The Theory of Abstract Motion* (1671), sec. 17, in *Philosophical Papers and Letters,* trans. Leroy E. Loemker, 2d ed. (Dordrecht: Reidel, 1969), p. 141.

lar explanations of physical events. But, at the level of basic metaphysical understanding of the nature of matter and motion, the Cartesian
attempt to keep the material world free of anything soul-like is
inadequate (chapters 19–22).

Spinoza's use of the concept of *conatus* retains some of the Cartesian
views rejected by Leibniz. For Spinoza, as for Descartes, what pertains
to mind remains separate from what pertains to matter. There are no
spiritual, soul-like principles in his explanations of matter and motion. There are no final causes. The nature and functioning of body is
to be explained without reference to mind. Neither motion nor indi-
viduation involves the presence in bodies of anything soul-like. Mind
and matter retain their utter separateness in Spinoza's system, although they are no longer substances but different attributes, each
expressing fully the same substance. But, although bodies are supposed to be understood without reference to minds and their properties, *conatus*—with its apparently anomalous associations with striving,
effort, endeavor—remains central to his treatment of both bodies and
minds.

Spinoza identifies *conatus* with the actual essence of individual
bodies. But, if we do shed from the notion of *conatus* all connotations
of mind, what have we left? The identification, as well as being
puzzling in its own right, may at first seem inconsistent with what we
have already seen of Spinoza's treatment of the individuality of bodies.
For we seem to have been offered two accounts of the essence of a
bodily individual. From his digression on the nature of bodies in Part
Two, it seems that the form of an individual consists in a certain ratio
of motion and rest. On the other hand, we are now told it consists in
the thing's "endeavour to persist in being." But, by treating these
answers as complementary, we get a clearer grasp of the implications
of Spinoza's treatment of individual bodies.

The suggestion that a thing's essence consists in its own endeavor to
persist in being seems at first sight paradoxical. It is of course plausible
to see some connections between the two: for a thing to continue to

exist it must have its essence intact. It is in the light of our understanding of a thing's essence—of what it is—that we know under what circumstances it would cease to exist. But it does seem strange to identify what the thing is with its endeavor to persist in being, for surely the thing must be what it is independent of that endeavor. In keeping itself in being, it keeps in being whatever is its essence. And it is through knowing its essence—knowing what it is—that we know what will count as success or failure in its endeavor to continue to exist.

But for Spinoza this striving is not to be construed as something the individual does. Strictly, there is no agent here, no subject identifiable independent of the striving. That a ratio of motion and rest comes to exist and is maintained is what it is for there to be an individual. So the relation between *conatus* and ratio of motion and rest can be stated as follows: the *conatus* of a thing consists in the maintenance of a certain ratio of motion and rest. This is the actuality of the thing—its "actual essence." It is what it is for that individual to exist. There is no suggestion that the striving is an activity performed by an independently identifiable individual. The activity is inextricably tied to the existence of the individual; it is not something in which the individual can be coherently said to engage. Nor is it strictly correct to say that an individual *has* a certain proportion of motion and rest. Rather, there being an individual consists in there being such a proportion. The individual exists just as long as the proportion is preserved, and to expect the continued existence of the individual is to expect the preservation of the proportion. And this is something that involves not just what goes on within the bodily superficies of what we, with our more traditional ways of thinking of individuals, would identify as an individual body. It involves, as we have seen, the pressure of conflicting forces from outside those superficies. What Spinoza retains of the Hobbesian notion of *conatus* is the picture of the material world as pulsating with the 'struggles' of conflicting forces. What is shed—and this is the crucial difference from Leibniz's version of *conatus*—is all idea of the "endeavor" as an activity performed by an independently identifiable individual. The ethical implications of this way of thinking of individuality become clearer in Spinoza's treatment of the individuality of human minds.

Self-Knowledge and the Union of Mind and Body

For Spinoza individual minds are no more substances than are individual bodies. But it is harder here to give content to the idea of individuality without substance. There is for minds as such no ana- logue of the ratio of motion to rest in bodies. But Spinoza's view of the mind-body relation allows his physics of bodies to provide a basis also for the individuality of minds. A mind is the individual it is by being the idea of a particular body, and it knows itself only through aware- ness of the bodily modifications of which it is the idea. This, however, is not the whole story of the mind's individuality. It is in the exertion of its own *conatus* that the mind's freedom and virtue reside. Although the content of that *conatus* cannot be stated without reference to the body, the mind's *conatus* is not at the mercy of the body's vicissitudes.

Spinoza's rejection of the status of substance, which was such a crucial feature of the Cartesian mind, has profound consequences. Whereas the Cartesian self was the epistemological center of the world—the luminous point from which knowledge radiates—this cen- tral position in Spinoza's system is held by the mind of God, conceived as the interconnected totality of modes of thought expressing the power of substance under that attribute. The individual mind becomes an idea in this totality. Like the body, of which it is the idea, the mind is integrated into wider systems that correspond in their totality to the universe as a unified whole. The power of substance is fully expressed in each of these systematically interconnected totalities of matter and mind, each mapping the other.

This view of the human mind as but one idea in the infinite intellect of God is at first sight even more bizarre than the human body's alleged containment in larger individuals, reaching up to the universe as a whole. Indeed it seems, as Spinoza himself acknowledges, a preposterous claim—a point on which his readers can be expected to "come to a halt, and think of many things which will given them pause" (11P11S). It seems to deprive us of all sense of our identity as autonomous knowers. When we say that the human mind perceives this or that, we are, according to Spinoza, saying that God has this or that idea (11P11C).

Spinoza could not be said to have overestimated the counter-intuitiveness of this view of the mind. At this point, Hegel seems fully justified in his perception of Spinoza's philosophy as threatening individual selfhood. The secure sense of the self as an autonomous knower is shattered. The self becomes a mere idea in a 'mind' not its own. But here, as with his treatment of bodies, Spinoza, having severed the links between individuality and substance, now reconstructs individuality without substance. To say that the human mind is an idea in the mind of God is just to express, with respect to the attribute of thought, the equivalent of the inclusion of bodies in a totality of material modes. Yet the ramifications for minds do seem more disconcerting. From within an intellectual tradition imbued with the spirit of the Cartesian view of the mind as ultimate arbiter of knowledge, it is difficult not to "come to a halt" at the claim that the mind is itself an idea whose adequacy needs to be assessed. Contemporary self-consciousness has been more strongly influenced by Descartes than by Spinoza. And our sharply contoured Cartesian minds balk at the apparent fluidity of Spinozistic mental individuals. But Spinoza gives back, in a new form, what he has taken away.

Individuality, we have seen, centers on the idea of a union of bodies, in a special sense. The component parts of bodies are constrained to agree among themselves in a ratio of motion and rest, the preservation of which depends on and resists the impinging of external forces. Differences between bodies involve the play of contrary forces. This means that the continued existence of an individual depends not just on what goes on within the bodily superficies of what we would regard as an individual body, but on the pressure of conflicting forces from outside. The corresponding truth about minds is that they are not ideas of self-contained material things but rather states of confused awareness of what is happening in the universe as a whole. Our ideas of other bodies involve the nature of our own bodies as well. In perceiving our bodies, we perceive together with them "a great many bodies." And our ideas of external bodies indicate the condition of our own bodies as much as—indeed more than—the nature of external bodies (IIP16Dem, with C1 and C2). Our awareness of ourselves thus emerges from a bodily awareness that cannot but be confused, for it involves awareness of resonances and disharmonies between bodies. The mind is itself a confused idea. It is, in Spinoza's expression, an "inadequate" idea of body—fragmented and partial. Of itself, considered independently of other ideas, it lacks the completeness that gives "adequate" ideas their truth. To say that the human mind perceives a thing only "partially, or inadequately" is to say that God has the idea of that thing insofar as "he also has the idea of another thing together with the human Mind" (IIP11C). The mind's immersion in the totality of modes of thought means that it lacks a standpoint from which it could readily have "adequate" understanding either of other things or of itself.

To be self-aware, then, is not to direct attention on an intellectual object—there to be known, independent of awareness of body. It is, rather, a refining of the direct sensory awareness of body. For Descartes such bodily awareness went beyond the awareness of self. Sensation involved the mind's turning toward body—a relationship between two supposedly distinct things. The Cartesian mind, intent on knowing how things really are, must shed the intrusions of the senses and imagination to devote itself to purely intellectual, clear, and distinct ideas. But there are deep problems with this approach. Descartes seems in fact to have two different and inconsistent accounts of sensation.

From some passages it seems that he thinks of sensation as a confused form of thought, inferior to the clear and distinct variety, but continuous with, and transformable into, the preferred kind of thinking. Thus, in his discussion of the piece of wax in the Second Meditation, the mind is seen as passing along a continuum from confused to clear perception. The perception of the wax is a "purely mental scrutiny" that can be imperfect or confused, as it was before, or clear and distinct, as it is now, depending on how carefully one concentrates on what the wax is. Here sensation seems to be confused thought about body, transformable through reflection into clear and distinct ideas. But in other passages, in the Sixth Meditation and in the *Passions of the Soul*, sensation seems rather to be a direct awareness of body, differing from pure thought not just in degree of clarity but in its object—something bodily rather than mental. Descartes, under the influence of a causal interaction model of the mind-body relationship, moves between these two ways of thinking of sensation. Our ideas of matter are the same in nature as our ideas of the mental. Because they are ideas—the same kind of thing as our ideas of mind—they can be treated as confused *thought*. But they proceed not from mind but from body and are produced in mind by physical movements acting on the pineal gland. That is why they are *confused* thought.

This way of thinking of mind-body union as a causal relation between two quite different kinds of thing is of course not unproblematic, as has been pointed out by Princess Elizabeth, at the time, and by many since. At the point of connection, identified by Descartes as the pineal gland, the causal model seems to break down. Either we are left with a mysterious interaction between two kinds of substance with supposedly nothing in common, or we must at this point regard the mind as having a direct, nonmediated awareness of the state of the pineal gland. It is this later view of sensation as direct awareness of body that is developed in Spinoza's treatment of the mind as idea of the body. This view seems implicit in the *Passions of the Soul* account of the mind's relations with the pineal gland, an account that exists in some tension with the causal interaction model. Descartes shifts uneasily between a full causal interaction model—with all its attendant difficulties—and this undeveloped, more Spinozistic approach, according to which the content of specific mental states is provided by states of body that are their direct objects.

Spinoza's version of self-knowledge is grounded in the substantial unity of mind and matter. Since "substance thinking" and "substance extended" are but the one substance under different attributes, there must also be a unity of material modes and their corresponding ideas. A mode of extension and the idea of that mode are "one and the same thing, but expressed in two ways" (IIP7S). Knowledge begins as the sensory awareness of body. This awareness is mental and hence radically distinct from body. But it is an expression of the same reality that body expresses. Its object is not something mental but body itself. Self-knowledge can arise only from this bodily awareness. What we know in knowing ourselves is not a self-contained intellectual entity set over against a material world. Rather, self-awareness is a reflective dimension on our awareness of the world.

For Descartes knowledge starts from the mind's awareness of mental objects, from which it reasons its way out to knowledge of a corresponding external reality. For Spinoza it is the other way around. Self-awareness is generated out of the reflective awareness of body. This reversal of the direction of knowledge is a consequence of central metaphysical theses of Spinoza's philosophy. A mind knows itself only through being aware of bodily modifications, because it is in fact nothing but the idea of such modification—the expression under the attribute of thought of the same reality that is expressed also as body. It follows that self-knowledge must share the inevitable confusion of bodily awareness. It can never be complete, for our bodies are part of nature and our minds cannot grasp all their interconnections. The mind has only fragmentary inadequate understanding of body and hence only an inadequate understanding of itself. Its knowledge of itself, of its own body, and of external bodies is "confused" and "mutilated" (IIP29C). The Cartesian mind is completely knowable to itself regardless of the existence of body—the most accessible of all objects of knowledge. Spinoza's self-knowledge, in contrast, is mediated through bodily awareness and must share its inadequacy.

The human body, as we have seen, needs other bodies by which it is "as it were continually regenerated" (11P19Dem). And this interconnection of things is reflected in the "order and connection of ideas." The mind knows the body and, hence, itself only through "ideas of affection by which the Body is affected" (11P19 and Dem). So the mind, insofar as it is considered separately from the multitude of ideas of bodily modes, must be inadequate and confused. But what sense can we make of this? It comes naturally to us to think of the mind as what assesses inadequacy and endeavors to eliminate it. Can we think coherently of the mind as itself a confused idea? It does not help here to be told that the mind is not one of its own confused ideas but a confused idea in the mind of God. The problem is to reconcile our conception of the mind as the source of judgment with thinking of it as itself an item to be judged in relation to other ideas. We think of ourselves as autonomous knowing subjects. And Spinoza himself talks as if the mind is what has confused ideas. So the mind, it seems, is both the judger of confusion and something whose very being consists in confusion. To follow Spinoza here, we must both think of ourselves as knowing subjects, with particular perspectives on the world, and place ourselves outside that perspective, to think of relationships among ideas that include ourselves.

Here, as elsewhere, Spinoza jolts his readers by using familiar locutions that turn out to imply something quite unfamiliar. But the shift from construing the mind as knower to construing it as just an idea in the totality of thought is the natural consequence of his treatment of individuality. The mind, like the body, is not a self-contained entity only incidentally interacting with others. Yet its individuality is not an illusion. Like all confused ideas, the mind is isolated out from the totality of thought, alienated from its status as part of a whole, removed from the larger wholes in which its confusion might be overcome. But it is nonetheless a real whole in relation to lower parts of the hierarchy of individuals. Spinozistic ideas are inherently perspectival. If we overlook this and treat them as akin to perspective-free facts or propositions, we miss an important aspect of their "incompleteness." Ideas are incomplete not just in being only part of a totality, but in being what they are only by virtue of their relations to the totality. Self-awareness involves awareness of how our bodies are affected by the rest of the world and shares the "confused and mutilated" character of that bodily awareness. But those bodies are not simply registering perturbations, like antennas. They have their own characteristic forces and rhythms, which they transmit to other bodies. Bodily modifications form unities only through fragile synchronizations of forces, and self-knowledge reflects their vicissitudes.

The strangeness of this view of mind comes out in Spinoza's perplexing claim that the mind must be aware of everything that happens in the body of which it is the idea. "Whatever happens to the object of the idea constituting the human Mind must be perceived by the human Mind, or there will necessarily be an idea of that thing in the Mind; i.e., if the object of the idea constituting a human Mind is a body, nothing can happen in that body which is not perceived by the Mind" (11P12). It is an apparently preposterous claim. Omniscience about what happens in a body may be all very well for a divine intellect. But the ideas that are vehicles of this knowledge are also supposed to be the minds we know and love so well. It is not less counterintuitive to be told that the ideas are "inadequate." For there is surely a great deal that goes on in our bodies of which we cannot be said to have even inadequate knowledge. But the claim seems less outrageous if we keep in mind the parallels with the individuality of bodies. Self-awareness is not awareness of something whose limits can be independently circumscribed.

My awareness of my own body also involves, as we have seen,

awareness of other bodies. But, if bodily awareness is fragmentary and confused, it cannot yield any clear understanding of the borders between my body and external bodies. Bodily awareness refers partly to my own body and partly to those impinging bodies I perceive along with it. In the appendix to Part One of the *Ethics,* Spinoza gives examples of the errors that can arise from treating the putative knowledge that arises from these "modes of imagining" as indicating the nature of things rather than the constitution of the imagination. But although it can be a source of error, this lack of clear demarcation within our bodily awareness holds the key to understanding the mind's true nature as part of wider wholes. Its full implications emerge in Spinoza's treatment of *conatus* in later sections of the *Ethics.*

Meanwhile, if we are not to "come to a halt" completely, it is important to keep in mind that the bodily awareness Spinoza is describing in these sections of Part Two is a perspectival awareness from within the totality, not an understanding of bodies from a vantage point outside them. It has more in common with what we might now call our "body image" than with a detached awareness of an anatomical object. Spinoza is perhaps best seen as articulating here what we now regard as phenomenological aspects of bodily awareness—describing what our bodies are like as grasped from our own bodily perspective. From this first-person perspective, the limits of my body just *are* the limits of my bodily awareness, rather than the superficies of my body as an externally perceived spatial object. The unity of this phenomenological object arises from the synchronization of forces that Spinoza goes on to describe, nonphenomenologically, in his account of the physics of bodies, between Propositions 13 and 14 of Part Two. But the individual mind experiences these synchronized forces from the perspective of the body of which it is the idea; and this involves, as we shall see in his treatment of the passions, not only cognitive awareness but also affectivity. Spinoza's treatment of emotion, no less than his account of self-knowledge, begins in his discussion of the physics of bodies. Here in Part Two he is already preparing an account of self-knowledge that takes seriously the emotional dimensions of our perspectival awareness of bodies as parts of wholes.

So the "limits" of my bodily awareness are not set by the spatial borders of bodies construed as anatomical entities. We do not have to wrestle with our intuitions that a lot goes on within the superficies of our bodies of which we are not conscious. The individuality of my body is for Spinoza not determined by spatial borders. It is the individuality of my body that sets limits to my self-awareness, and that is not something with predefined contours. Understanding my body involves understanding my bodily powers and the ways in which they are strengthened or impeded through those of other bodies.

An individual mind, then, is not for Spinoza an independently existing whole, there to be adequately understood, whether by itself or through some way of knowing that remains inaccessible to it. Its reality consists in the reality of an inadequate idea—in an awareness of matter from within the totality of material modes. The mind is an inherently perspectival, direct awareness of body. With regard to the totality, the distinction between different ideas is just the distinction between different proportions of motion and rest among the bodily modifications that are their objects. Since those ratios are all interdependent, it might seem that with regard to the whole there are no individuals. But it makes no sense within Spinoza's system to think of a mind perceiving from that standpoint. The "mind of God" just is the totality, and human minds are located within it. If we imagine ourselves as having a perspective-free perception of the whole, it may seem that Spinoza is committed to rejecting individuality as an illusion produced by the distortions of inadequate modes of thought. Hegel, as Sartre comments in his discussion of Hegelian self-consciousness in *Being and Nothingness*,[8] was perhaps all too ready to adopt such a holistic stand-

8. Jean-Paul Sartre, *Being and Nothingness*, trans. Hazel E. Barnes (New York: Philosophical Library, 1956), Part 3, chap. 1, sec. 3, p. 243.

point. But for Spinoza it does not follow from the fact that individuality depends on perspectival perception that it is an illusion.

The Spinozistic mind is not an independently existing whole, there to be adequately grasped by some means of knowledge it does not itself possess. Its reality consists in the reality of inadequate ideas—in the awareness of body from within the totality of modes. The mind is an inherently perspectival awareness of body. The inadequacy of self-knowledge could be transcended only at the cost of our ceasing to exist. We can nonetheless, through transforming inadequate ideas into more adequate ones, come to greater self-knowledge. There is a paradox here, the details of which I will explore in later sections. Individual selfhood, it seems, resides in the mind's status as an inadequate idea. Yet by transforming inadequate ideas into more adequate ones, the mind is supposed to come to greater self-knowledge. This apparently paradoxical transformation is for Spinoza the path to freedom and virtue.

The Ethics of Individuality

Different commentators give different content to what is involved in a Spinozistic idea. Stuart Hampshire suggests that Spinoza's use of the term "idea" is wide enough to include what we would normally call an "assertion" or "proposition."[9] Roger Scruton complains that the term crosses two critical frontiers: that between concept and perception and that between concept and proposition.[10] Edwin Curley argues that the relation between thought and extension can be interpreted in terms of the identity of the world as the set of true propositions and the world as the set of facts.[11] To be part of a totality of thought is then a relatively straightforward matter: a human mind is a

9. Stuart Hampshire, *Spinoza* (Harmondsworth, U.K.: Penguin, 1987), p. 74.
10. Scruton, *Spinoza*, pp. 65–66.
11. Edwin Curley, *Spinoza's Metaphysics: An Essay in Interpretation* (Cambridge: Harvard University Press, 1969), p. 124.

subset of the totality of true propositions.[12] But it is then not easy to see what to make of Spinoza's claim that the mind has at any rate inadequate knowledge of all that happens to its body or what ethical significance such knowledge might have, even if we could attain it.[13] If, on the other hand, we emphasize the psychological aspect of ideas, it becomes difficult to see what he could possibly mean by their inclusion in a unified totality.

Spinoza in fact seems to move readily between the logical and psychological senses of "idea," without clearly distinguishing them. What for us seem quite disparate ways of thinking of ideas are for him on a continuum. This is partly due to his thinking of ideas, in opposition to Descartes, as active affirmations of body. Ideas for Spinoza are not "mute pictures on a panel" awaiting external affirmation or denial (11P49S2). This means that the mind, as idea of the body, is not a mere passive reflection of bodily states. Its individuality, as we have seen, parallels that of bodies. Indeed, since the mind is defined as idea of body, it can be seen as drawing its individuality from that of its body, although this of course is not a causal interaction. But thought, of which the mind is a mode, is an attribute relating directly to substance—an alternative expression of substance, mapping that of mat-

12. Ibid., p. 132.
13. For Curley, in *Spinoza's Metaphysics*, my body is a set of facts, my mind a set of propositions describing those facts (p. 127). The unacceptable consequence—that the mind is conscious of everything that goes on in the body—is avoided by insisting that consciousness demands not merely ideas but "ideas of ideas," which can be thought of as propositions about other propositions (pp. 127–29). However, as Curley points out in his later discussion of the point in *Behind the Geometrical Method* (pp. 71–72), Spinoza's discussion at 11P20–22 seems to imply that each mind contains an idea of each of its ideas and hence—if consciousness is equated with the presence of ideas of ideas—is conscious of all the states of its body. These issues are also perceptively discussed by Margaret Wilson in "Objects, Ideas, and 'Minds': Comments on Spinoza's Theory of Mind," in Richard Kennington, ed., *The Philosophy of Baruch Spinoza;* Studies in Philosophy and the History of Philosophy, vol. 7 (Washington, D.C.: Catholic University of America Press, 1980), pp. 103–20; and by Alan Donagan in *Spinoza* (Chicago: University of Chicago Press, 1989), pp. 125–30. I discuss the problems that arise from Spinoza's claim that the mind is aware of all that happens in the body more fully in Chapter 2, this volume.

ter. So, although it has the body as its object, the mind also belongs in a totality of thought that relates directly to substance.

The ethical implications of Spinoza's treatment of the mind come from the interactions between these two aspects of the mind-body relation—on the one hand the fact that the mind has the body as its object, on the other its independence, as a mode of thought directly related to substance. Mind's *conatus* is the endeavor to persist as an active articulation and affirmation of the body. But this *conatus* is not a mere passive reflection of the body's vicissitudes. As well as being mapped onto a segment of the material world, the mind is inserted into the totality of thought. This gives it, as it were, scope for expansion that is causally independent of the body. The mind strives to understand its own interconnections with other ideas. In doing so it comes to a clearer understanding of the body of which it is the idea. Rather than staying at the level of a mere passive awareness of body—as if it were a mute picture on a panel—it endeavors to become a more adequate idea of body, transforming itself from a passive picture to an active articulation.

Because thought and extension are not, as they were for Descartes, different substances but rather different attributes of the same substance, thought cannot go its own way in the manner allowed as a possibility in Descartes's play at skeptical doubt in the First Meditation. Thought cannot produce ideas for which there are no nonmental correlates. Every idea is the awareness of some bodily mode; but it may be an inadequate, incomplete awareness. The mind may, in the manner of the worm in the blood, be aware of something bodily in a way that gives that thing the distorted status of a whole. The idea may fail to affirm the bodily mode in a way that grasps it in its surrounding context, failing to see it as part of a whole. Its articulation of the bodily mode is then distorted. The mode is affirmed as a false individual, as a self-contained segment of reality, isolated out from the external forces that are the source of the body's continued existence as an individual, as well as of its vulnerability.

If the intrusion of external forces disrupts a body's characteristic rhythm, that body will cease to exist. But without exposure to external forces, the body could not sustain its characteristic ratio of motion to rest on which its individuality depends. The body's individuality depends on not being insulated from its environment. All this has its correlate for the mind. The mind's endeavor to affirm what contributes to the body's continued existence and well-being yields its own thriving—an increase in virtue and freedom. The body's interactions with its environment, as we have seen, can either impede or enhance its own power and activity. And the mind's *conatus* is expressed in the effort to imagine those things that increase or assist the body's power of acting (IIIP12). But because the mind is the idea of the body, this effort is also an endeavor to imagine those things that affirm the mind's own power of acting (IIIP54). The body's thriving or ailing is reflected in mind's transitions to greater or lesser states of activity.

Bodies are more or less powerful according to their capacity to sustain and benefit from a variety of activities without surrendering their own distinctive ratios of motion and rest. The superiority of the human body over others resides in the fact that it is "affected in a great many ways by external bodies, and is disposed to affect external bodies in a great many ways" (IIP14Dem). This makes it possible for the body to maintain its individuality throughout a wide variety of changes. And this too has its correlate for the well-functioning mind.

It is easy to ridicule Spinoza's treatment, in Parts Four and Five of the *Ethics*, of the correlations between bodily and mental thriving. But it makes sense, against the background of his treatments of the mind-body relation and of individuality, as a description of conditions that manifest an ill-functioning mind—conditions that derive from a false understanding of the mind's status, from a lack of self-knowledge. At the core of this failure to know ourselves is an inadequate understanding of individuality.[14] The human body cannot exist in isolation from

14. I give a fuller treatment of the ethical implications of the false understanding of individuality in section 5 of my "Spinoza's Version of the Eternity of the Mind," in Marjorie Grene and Debra Nails, eds., *Spinoza and the Sciences*, Boston Studies in the Philosophy of Science, vol. 91 (Dordrecht: Reidel, 1986), pp. 211–33.

the surrounding totality that provides and sustains its individuality. The isolated body would cease to exist. The mind, likewise, can exist as an individual only in the context of other modes of thought. But the mind, unlike the body, has open to it a false version of individuality. Minds, unlike bodies, can know what they are. And as well as being capable of knowledge they are capable of error. The mind can think of the body, and hence of itself, falsely—it can think of itself as substance.

The state of error is the state of fragmentary, incomplete awareness. In this state, the mind has direct sensory awareness of bodily modifications but lacks understanding of their context. It is in a similar state to that illustrated in Spinoza's description of the worm in the blood. The mind in error remains in existence. For it remains the awareness of an actually existing individual body, however wrongly that awareness may conceive its object. But the mind does not grasp the basis of the body's individuality and hence does not fully understand its own individuality either. This lack of understanding restricts its power and limits its freedom. The tendency to isolate individual bodies—one's own and others—out from the totality is for Spinoza connected with states of destructive passion, of bondage. In the state of passion, the mind lacks adequate understanding of the causes of bodily modification. Ignorance of the causes of our pleasures and pains breeds obsession. The mind in the grip of passion loses its capacity to enjoy a wide range of activities. Its affirmation becomes limited to things it conceives, wrongly, as the sole cause of its pleasures and pains—particular segments of the world that are given distorted status as self-contained individuals. The mind takes its own individuality to depend on falsely construed individuals, failing to grasp that they are but parts of wider wholes. In failing to understand the objects on which it depends, the mind fails too to understand its own interconnections with wider wholes. In failing to understand our loves and hates we fail to understand ourselves.[15]

15. For an interesting discussion of Spinoza's analysis of obsessive love and its implications for self-knowledge, see Amélie Rorty, "Spinoza on the Pathos of

Part of Nature

In such states of error, based on false conceptions of individuality, the mind remains part of a whole. But minds can, and for the most part do, live without realizing their real nature. Such minds live without transcending the limitations of inadequate forms of knowledge. In cultivating the higher forms of knowledge, the mind comes to understand the body—of which it is the idea—and hence itself as part of a whole. This involves being the idea of a body capable of sustaining a great number of activities. Such a body is best able to withstand being placed in bondage by a rival *conatus*. And the minds associated with such bodies are "least troubled by evil affects," that is, by "affects contrary to our nature" (vP39Dem).

The mind that manages to affirm bodies as parts of wider contexts is the idea of a body engaged in a large variety of activities without being reduced to passivity. Such a mind is open to the intrusion of the rest of the world without having its own activity subdued. Human life for Spinoza is a constant struggle between activity and passivity, autonomy and dependence, freedom and bondage—a struggle to remain in the state of activity and power in which individuality resides. The mind is under constant threat of succumbing to a false individuality— of seeing individuals as essentially independent of the rest of the world, as individual substances. This is a metaphysical error that Spinoza sees as breeding moral error. To see interaction with the rest of reality as incidental to a thing's individuality—to see things only as 'wholes'—is the underlying illusion built into obsessive loves and hates. True freedom of mind, and with it true understanding of individuality, is to be attained only through the apprehension of truth involved in the higher forms of knowledge. The mind's active affirmation of reality through adequate knowledge, Spinoza sees as a vulnerable force, with dubious power against the frequently overwhelming external forces that put the mind into bondage—a force, nonetheless,

Idolatrous Love and the Hilarity of True Love," in Robert C. Solomon and Kathleen M. Higgins, eds., *The Philosophy of (Erotic) Love* (Lawrence: University Press of Kansas, 1991), pp. 352–71.

that contains the germ of freedom. We will see in later chapters how this freedom is attained.

Self-Knowledge and the Ideal of Completeness

Descartes thought that in knowing ourselves we also know how the world is. The Cartesian mind is a self-contained substance, existing independently of all else except for God. It knows itself by turning away from "external" objects, whose existence is dubitable, to contemplate itself, whose existence cannot be doubted. The mind would be exactly as it is even if the rest of the world, including its own body, were not there at all. But the content of Cartesian knowledge does not match this utter existential separateness. It might be expected that Descartes's method of doubt, focusing as it does on the self while the rest of the world is left in abeyance, would leave thought thoroughly impoverished. But, although the existence of the self is completely separated out from the rest of the world, it has an exceedingly rich inner life. In focusing on itself as object of knowledge, the mind is really deprived of nothing. For what at first seems a direct awareness of external objects—an awareness that the mind must forfeit in the method of doubt—turns out, on reflection, to be self-knowledge. The nonmaterial mind replicates in its ideas the basic structure of the world so that, in knowing itself, it knows how the world is.

These connections between knowing ourselves and knowing the world are supposed to be demonstrated by Descartes's ingeniously constructed analysis of the piece of wax in the Second Meditation. He begins from an apparent paradox. The attempt to doubt everything has shown that we do not know with certainty that material things exist. Yet, it seems, we know their nature with absolute certainty. On the other hand, we know with absolute certainty that our minds exist, while having no clear knowledge of their nature. This disparity between certainty of existence and certainty about the nature of what exists seems counterintuitive. And the analysis of the awareness of the

wax is meant to remove this counterintuitive separation of the understanding of natures from the affirmation of existence. Our knowledge
of the nature of the wax, which seems to come through the senses, is
shown to be in fact nonsensory awareness, pertaining to the purely
intellectual character of the mind. So it is not just our minds that are
known through the exercise of pure intellect; contrary to appearances,
we know the rest of the world in that way too. The appearance that
what we 'know' through the senses is more clearly grasped than what
we know through nonsensory, purely intellectual awareness is thus
mistaken. Moreover, Descartes argues, there is no knowledge that we
can have about the world which does not add to the knowledge we
have of ourselves. Far from the self being a hazy, elusive object of
knowledge, it is the paradigm of clear knowledge. There is nothing
more easily known than the mind.

The structure of Descartes's argument for the claim that the mind
understands the nature of the wax through pure thought rather than
through the senses is clear enough, even if it leaves us unpersuaded.
Those aspects of the wax that are the proper objects of sensory
awareness can be removed without interrupting our continued perception of the wax itself. Our understanding of the wax involves perceiving it as capable of undergoing a wide range of changes in determinate
properties such as color, smell, or shape. But sensory awareness is
confined to confrontation with a succession of determinate states,
none of which can make us aware of the possibility of the others. It
follows, Descartes argues, that it cannot be by means of the senses that
I know the wax. Nor can it be by means of the imagination. For the
possibilities of change in the determinate properties of the wax are
infinite, but the imagination cannot "compass the infinitude." It must
be by means of an act of pure intellect alone that I know the wax. But
the wax that is thus known is the same as he has believed it to be all
along, although it is now grasped through a clear and distinct perception rather than, as formerly, through a confused one.

Descartes is attempting to transform the paradigm of clear and distinct perception from sensory presentation to thought. He argues that the mind's initial conviction that its sensations are clear, whereas what it perceives through thought—such as its own existence—is vague and indefinite, is an illusion. This transformation is closely related to a deeper one. Understanding and senses are no longer distinguished as different parts of the soul. There is no longer any dualism within the soul. All knowledge becomes purely intellectual, although some of it is purer than the rest. The thinking mind, he stresses in his replies to Gassendi on the Second Meditation, is not part of the soul but "the thinking soul in its entirety" (AT VII, 356; Cott. II, 246). He elaborates this theme of the unity of the soul, now identified with the mind, in the *Passions of the Soul* (Part I, art. 47; AT XI, 364–65; Cott. I, 346). There is within us but one soul, and this soul has within it no diversity of parts. It is both sensitive and rational, and all its appetites are volitions. It is an error, Descartes continues, to treat the different functions of the soul as if they were persons playing different, usually conflicting, roles. The error arises from our failure to distinguish properly the functions of the soul from those of the body. Where the earlier philosophical tradition had talked of nonrational aspects or elements of the soul, Descartes insists that we should attribute to the body alone everything we can find in us opposed to reason.

Cartesian dualism is not a dualism between parts of the soul, but solely between the soul—now identified with the mind—and the body. What is nonrational is no longer part of the soul; it pertains to body. This relocation of dualism extends the scope of what can be subjected to scientific explanation. The operation of the senses, rather than being seen as a function of the human soul, rejoins the material world, where it can be explained in the same kind of way as the rest of nature. At the same time, what is purely intellectual is separated entirely from the scope of scientific explanation.

The separation of the operations of pure thought from the objects of scientific explanation gives a straightforward but negative content to the claim that the analysis of the knowledge of the wax also clarifies for us the nature of the mind. It adds to our knowledge of the mind by making us realize what mind is not and how different it is from body. But Descartes thinks something much stronger than this has also emerged. We are now supposed to have something more than just a clearer conception of the nature of matter and hence of what mind is not. We have not gained merely a better understanding of how different mind is from matter. Our improved understanding of the wax is supposed to give us an improved understanding of the actual nature of the mind. We are now supposed to realize that we in fact know mind much more clearly than we know body. But it is by no means obvious why this should be so. All the reasons that contribute to the knowledge of the wax, or any other body, says Descartes, are yet better proofs of the nature of my mind. It seems clear enough that every exercise of the mind confirms its knowledge of its own existence. But why should it be the case that every such exercise of the mind adds to its knowledge of its own nature? Descartes expressed surprise at Gassendi's puzzlement on this point, insisting that the one thing cannot be proved without the other, and ridiculing Gassendi's apparent need for a kind of chemical investigation of the mind, as if he expects to be told what color or smell or taste it has, or the proportions of salt, sulphur, and mercury from which it is made up. In contrast to that supposedly confused conception of what is involved in knowing the nature of the mind, Descartes's own account of it is astonishingly simple. We can distinguish many attributes in the wax—that it is white, that it is hard, that it can be melted, and so on—and correspondingly many attributes in the mind—that it can know hardness, and so on. So for whatever attributes we know in wax, we know corresponding attributes in the mind. And this applies not only to wax but to all the material things we know. Hence the nature of the mind is what we know best of all (AT VII, 360; Cott. II, 248–49).

There is much that is puzzling about Descartes's transposition of the attributes of the wax into correlated attributes of the mind that knows it.[16] Descartes's point is not just that the mind comes to know its own general powers through exercising them, coming to understand itself as a being with the general power of thinking. Through its knowledge of the material world it comes to know itself as, in part, a replica of that world. Many of our mental contents do not pertain to body. But insofar as our knowledge is directed to the material world, our minds replicate in themselves the structure of that world. What we know in knowing matter is at the same time our nature as minds. Thus all knowledge of the world is also self-knowledge. A "chemical" analysis of the mind is not only impossible but also superfluous. For we already know our minds in knowing the rest of the world. To think we need further analysis of the mind is to misconstrue mind's relationship to the world.

We can see emerging here an idea of self-knowledge as a reflective version of our knowledge of the world. It is an idea that will be more clearly articulated in Spinoza's version of self-knowledge. But there it will be combined with a full acceptance of the idea that mind knows body directly—that mind is the direct awareness of body. In Descartes's version, the idea of self-knowledge as reflective knowledge of matter exists uneasily with the idea of mind as a self-contained substance, causally interacting with matter. And this presents a problem. If knowledge of the world is indeed knowledge of a self that is substance, it is by no means clear what is added to the self's knowledge when it knows that matter does indeed exist outside it. What is added to our ideas of body when we know that body exists independently of mind? Descartes's intellectual substance is so complete that it is difficult to see what difference the existence of the "external" world can really make to it. With mind a complete replica of the external world, what need have we of that world? What is it exactly that belief in the nondeceiving God salvages?

16. For a discussion of the internal difficulties in Descartes's account, see Margaret Dauler Wilson's *Descartes: Ego Cogito Ergo Sum* (London: Routledge and Kegan Paul, 1978), pp. 92–99.

Descartes's veracious God assures a complete matching between adequate ideas and matter. But he seems also to have a more important role within the Cartesian system: he keeps mind and matter apart. It is only through his good offices that the mind knows that there is indeed a material existence, different from its own, whose structure, however, mirrors perfectly the nonmaterial natures it discerns within itself. The world contributes nothing to the mind's understanding of the nature of the body. Hence it offers no resistance to the mind's power of knowing the world. Although the mind's primary and, in a sense, only direct object of knowledge is itself, the veracity of God ensures that there are no limits to the extent of its knowledge of the world—a world, however, that seems to remain strangely incidental to that knowledge. The independent existence of the world—despite the role of the veracious God—has become curiously attenuated. Despite the assurance of its substantial difference from mind, it seems curiously lacking in substance. What gives it density—its resistance to mind, its capacity to reduce the activity of the mind to passivity—is the causal impact of body through sensation. But that, as we have seen, does not give us knowledge of the nature of things but only of their existence.

Clear and distinct ideas inform us of the nature of body. But it is the reality of confused perception—sensation—that assures us of the existence of body and hence of the separate existence of mind and matter. So it is only the "intermingling" of mind and body that enables us to know that mind and matter are in fact two separately existing substances. Awareness of the existence and of the nature of matter—apparently separate at the beginning of the wax passage—now come together again. The mind, reasoning about the fact that it has confused sensations, knows that there is an external world and, given the veracity of God, that the world is as it judges it to be through clear and distinct ideas. Our originally unreflective belief in the existence of a world independent of mind turns out to be right after all. But, in the process, our understanding of the nature of body has been entirely transformed. In coming to reaffirm our basic beliefs about the material world, we have transformed our conceptions of knowledge and of its objects. We are not back where we began. What we know to exist is not the commonsense world from which we began in the First Meditation—not that familiar commonsense world in which we experience colors, shapes, the sweetness of honey, the agreeable scent of flowers. It is rather a world of mathematical properties—a crystalline structure, corresponding to our clear and distinct ideas. Our senses, Descartes insists, are not guides to the nature of things but only to our being able to find our way around the world without being destroyed by it—guides to the avoidance of pain, the sustaining of well-being. Sensuous awareness is an irrelevant and distorting intrusion in the enterprise of gaining adequate knowledge of how things are.

Descartes equates theoretical knowledge with clear and distinct ideas, rightly ordered. The senses are not involved in understanding the material world. They guide us in the pursuit of well-being and the avoidance of pain, serving our interests as practical agents rather than as theoretical knowers. This exclusion of sensation from knowledge is something of an embarrassment for the Cartesian system. For, as we have seen, it is only the reality of sensation that can ultimately assure Cartesian knowers that the material world is indeed there to be known. If the senses cannot give us knowledge of *what* exists, how are they capable of informing us of the existence of those things known only through intellect? The knowledge of existence here seems a sophisticated piece of knowledge, not just experiences, say, of bumping into things. The proof of the existence of matter in the Sixth Meditation makes it clear that, despite God's veracity, pure thought cannot take us beyond solipsistic consciousness. Our knowledge of the reality of matter rests ultimately on that confused sensory awareness which is nonetheless rejected as extraneous to the nature of knowledge. The world, construed independently of sensation, remains a substanceless projection of pure theoretical consciousness.

All this results in a split within the Cartesian self. On the one hand,

Descartes equates himself with the intellectual substance known through pure consciousness. On the other, he insists, in the Sixth Meditation, that this self is not lodged in its body like a pilot in a vessel but is so intermingled with it as to form with it one being. Sensuous awareness is essential to a composite self. The very existence of the self of everyday awareness, like the commonsense world of sensible qualities in which it has its being, is a product of the intermingling of mind and matter. But he also wants this intermingling to be nonessential to the self as knower. So there is for Descartes a split between the concerns of the self as knower and its more mundane practical dealings with the world, which cannot be conducted in the state of rarified clear and distinct consciousness appropriate to pure thought. What is demanded by the practical activities of life, he stresses in Part III of the *Discourse on Method,* is very different from what is expected of us as knowers. The bulk of life is rightly given over to the sway of senses and imagination—to that middle, muddled zone of confused perception where mind and body intermingle.

Descartes comes nearest a resolution of this troublesome split between the self as knower and as inhabitant of the commonsense world in his disconcerting remarks to Princess Elizabeth, in a letter of 28 June 1643 (AT III, 690), about the priorities of a rationally lived life. The rarified air of metaphysical understanding, he there suggests, is an improper climate for everyday life. The glimpses it affords of the nature of things are rare and difficult to sustain. They nonetheless provide an essential framework for secure enjoyment of the sensuous, unplagued by doubts about the reliability of knowledge. But this neat Cartesian arrangement for reconciling our metaphysical self-understanding with our status as practical agents is extremely fragile. The commonsense world of sensory confusion rests on a crystalline structure of pure thought in correspondence with unmingled matter. But that structure remains remote from the commonsense world for which it is supposed to provide a foundation. The knowing self must endeavor to align itself with the structures of pure thought, to render itself translucent as an ordered set of clear and distinct ideas replicating the metaphysical structure of the world. Only by removing itself from the confusion that is the reality of the commonsense world can it secure the foundations of that world. Clear and distinct consciousness is divorced—by the demands of the Cartesian system itself—from the world of ordinary experience in ways that reinforce the irrelevance of philosophy to ordinary life.

The price to be paid for Cartesian purity of consciousness is the separation of self from world. If the self is indeed an intellectual substance, complete unto itself, it cannot also be incomplete without matter. Its life in the zone of sensory awareness cannot but be an accidental intermingling of mind and extraneous matter that does not belong to its essence. If true perception is to be attained by shedding the intrusions of body, what is really added by knowing that matter exists? Even at the height of its self-confidence, the Cartesian self cannot be fully assured of its strength as an autonomous knower. The price of its successful matching to an independent objective world, via the will of the veracious God, is the apparent irrelevance of that world to its knowledge. The dilemma of the Cartesian self thus resides in its status as self-contained substance. This is the source of its supposed autonomy as knower; but, at the same time, it is the source of its separation from the world it purports to know. With the subsequent disintegration of the metaphysical machinery necessary to secure its contact with the world, its essential isolation becomes apparent. But even within the confines of seventeenth-century rationalism the dilemmas of the Cartesian self were apparent to Spinoza.

It is its very lack of the status of substance that makes the Spinozistic self less vulnerable than the Cartesian self in its relation with the world. If a self thinks itself, wrongly, to be an intellectual substance, it is more prone to feel cut off from the world. If a mind clearly understands that it is a mode, it understands also that it is interconnected with the rest of reality. The Cartesian self is fated to the hopeless attempt to insert itself back into a world from which it has been metaphysically separated. Precisely because it is complete in itself, the self is isolated from the rest of the world. Its replication of the world is also its imprisonment. It is a 'complete' individual that must attempt the impossible task of locking itself back into the world. Its craving for union with the rest of nature haunts Cartesian consciousness, and so too does fear of the collapse of the metaphysical and theological apparatus on which it depends for contact with its 'external' world.

The Spinozistic self, in contrast, is immersed in the whole of nature, and its self-knowledge consists in becoming ever more deeply and reflectively aware of that truth. A Spinozistic mode might, of course, fail—even without wrongly believing itself to be a substance—to realize the implications of its modal status. But, to the extent that it does, it avoids the predicament of the Cartesian self. It does not have to try to insert itself into the world. We have seen that for Spinoza the mind is, as a mode of thought, radically different from bodily modes. But this distinction does not set up a gulf between self and world; and, as we shall see in the next chapter, the reflecting Spinozistic mind cannot take skepticism seriously. The self consists in ideas of matter, and it struggles to articulate its selfhood within a total idea of that world of which it is an essential part. The mind is of its nature directly aware of the world; the only question is how adequate this awareness will become. Nor do the dilemmas posed by sensation in the Cartesian philosophy arise for Spinoza. Sensation is not a distorting and irrelevant intrusion into the mind's clarity. It is basic to knowledge. Although it is transcended through the cultivation of reason, it remains on a continuum with the higher forms of knowledge. There is no radical discontinuity, as there was for Descartes, between clear and distinct scientific consciousness and the confused perceptions of everyday life. They are not polarized, as they are for Descartes, by being superimposed on the dichotomy of mind and matter. There is for Spinoza no analogue of the separation of the concerns of pure intellect from mind's concern with its intermingling with body.

For Spinoza bodily awareness is not an extraneous intrusion into intellectual life. The self is not a pure ego that happens to be trapped in a body. It is the articulation of bodily awareness, and its self-awareness emerges from an increasingly adequate understanding of body. This is an account of the mind that emphasizes, rather than resists, its involvement with the perturbations of body. Body is not alien to the Spinozistic mind. And its pursuit of theoretical knowledge, as we will see in later chapters, has a continuity that Descartes's philosophy denied with its pursuit of bodily well-being.

TWO

O

Knowledge, Truth, and Error

Although we do not have to see Spinoza's philosophy as collapsing individuals into an all-encompassing whole, there is nonetheless some basis for Hegel's unease about his monism. For it is true that, if we confine our attention to what can be grasped through reason, there is no differentiation between Spinoza's individuals. Our capacity to distinguish between them presupposes that we are perceiving through sense or imagination, although it is only through the higher forms of knowledge that we understand what we are perceiving. Spinoza, after all, is a rationalist. He exalts reason over the lesser faculties. Must we then not accept that, for him, as for Descartes, the real world is the world as it is perceived through reason? If individuals are not there independently of sensation, is not that to say that they are not there at all? And, if the individual mind itself is not there independently of sensation, does not this make Hegel's fears all the more warranted? Such a reading is indeed endorsed by some more recent commentators, including Roger Scruton, who argues that for Spinoza true perception and freedom demand that we rise above the "illusory perspective" of inadequate ideas to "the absolute viewpoint which is God's."[1] But this is too rigid an interpretation of Spinoza's rationalism.

1. Roger Scruton, *Spinoza* (Oxford: Oxford University Press, 1986), p. 73.

We have seen that for Spinoza the reality of the mind consists in the reality of inadequate ideas—in the awareness of body from within the totality of ideas of body. The individual mind is a direct, inherently perspectival awareness of body. If reason is regarded as transcending inferior modes of knowledge to grasp what is real, as distinct from mere appearance, then individuals do seem, as Hegel feared, to slip through Spinoza's net. But this is a misleading picture of Spinoza's treatment of the relations between reason and the lower faculties of sense and imagination, underestimating just how radical is his transformation of Cartesian rationalism. Reason, in Spinoza's version of it, although clearly superior to sense and imagination, does not transcend them in the Cartesian way.

What then is Spinoza's version of reason? In Part Two of the *Ethics* he distinguishes it from the lesser forms of awareness by its access to adequate ideas. This point he shares with Descartes. But for Spinoza sensory awareness retains a central role in adequate knowledge. And we have seen too that the presence of body plays a very different role in his account of sensation. For Descartes the body plays an instrumental role in bringing mental representations to the mind's awareness. For Spinoza sensation involves the direct presence of body to mind. It is not awareness of a mental representation produced by body, but a direct awareness of body itself. Like Descartes, he thinks that the ideas of sensation and imagination are inadequate, in contrast to the adequacy of the ideas of reason. But the direct awareness of body that they involve, while it is a source of error, is also the precondition and basis for reason and intuition—the higher forms of knowledge. The possibility of reason and the possibility of error have a common base in the powers of the human body.

The mind's capacity for reason rests on the complexity of the human body, which makes it capable of retaining traces of affections after their immediate activity has subsided. In its lowest form this power of imagining modifications after they have ceased gives rise to the blurring of images that Spinoza regards as the bad way of forming universals (11P40S1). Such notions, in contrast to the good universals, the "common notions" of reason, are formed differently by different minds according to the different dispositions of the bodies of which they are ideas. Those who have more often regarded men's stature with wonder will understand by the word *man* an animal of erect stature. Others will form different common images of a human being—as an animal capable of laughter, a featherless biped, or a rational animal. Such universals, because they arise from confused sense perceptions without the order of the intellect, do not transcend "knowledge from random experience" (11P40S2). The power of imagination, based in the body's capacity to retain traces, makes possible inadequate knowledge. But it also makes possible the good universals, the common notions through which we grasp what different bodily modifications have in common, thus coming to more adequate understanding of ourselves as ideas of those bodies. Through reason the mind is determined internally, rather than externally through fortuitous encounters with things, to regard a number of things at once (11P29S). But this capacity for reason depends on its having available a multiplicity of bodily modifications in which it can discern similarity and difference. The highest power of reason thus depends on the same bodily power manifested in imagination.

What makes the human mind superior to other ideas then is the capacity of its object, the complex structure of the human body. Other bodies lack the capacity to retain modifications after the impingements on them of other bodies have subsided. For them there is no transition from the ideas of actual bodily modification to the understanding of them through common notions. It is this notion of a transition between levels of ideas that is crucial to understanding Spinoza's treatment of consciousness and self-knowledge. The mere presence of "ideas of ideas" does not guarantee consciousness. For that applies to the ideas of all bodily modification. The idea of an idea is its form "insofar as this is considered as a mode of thinking without relation to the object." And the idea of the mind and the mind itself are one and the same thing, just as the mind and its object, the body, are one and the same (11P21S). This shadowing of ideas by ideas of them might seem to suggest that Spinoza thinks all bodies are animate. Edwin Curley has pointed out that, even if it commits Spinoza to thinking that all things are, in some sense, living, it does not commit him to saying that the souls of very simple bodies engage in anything like a human mental life.[2] The human mind, unlike the ideas of other bodies, can appropriate to itself the unity between ideas and ideas of ideas, thus perceiving "not only the affections of the Body, but also the ideas of those affections" (11P22). Spinoza draws a cryptic distinction in this context between different ways in which ideas can be said to be "in God." Ideas of ideas of human bodily affections are in God "insofar as he constitutes the essence of the human Mind" (11P22Dem). Ideas of ideas of other bodily affections, although they are, like all ideas, in God, are not there as constituting the essence of a mind. The difference is grounded in degree of bodily complexity. It is the capacity of our bodies to retain modifications in the absence of their immediate causes that makes it possible for our minds to understand our bodies and hence ourselves. Our common notions are grounded in bodily awareness. Self-knowledge depends on the continued anchoring of the common notions in awareness of body. The common notions cannot of themselves reach individuals.

All this means that for Spinoza, unlike Descartes, the possibility of error is linked with that of the higher forms of knowledge. In knowing through common notions we know what bodies have in common. But this knowledge is grounded in awareness of what our own bodies have in common with others. Reason is grounded in imagination and, as we shall see later, also in affectivity. Our bodily structure makes it possible for our minds to know those bodies and hence themselves. But, as ideas of those complex bodies, our minds are inherently fragmented, and hence their ideas are inherently liable to inadequacy and error.

2. Edwin Curley, *Behind the Geometrical Method: A Reading of Spinoza's "Ethics"* (Princeton: Princeton University Press, 1988), p. 73.

Knowledge, Truth, and Error

The Nature of Error

Spinozistic individuality is connected with the inadequacy of ideas. But I have argued that this does not make it an illusion. Knowledge through common notions can be knowledge of individuals only because it retains continuity with the "inadequate" ideas of sense or imagination. But there are problems in knowing what to make of Spinoza's version of inadequacy that parallel those we have already seen in relation to individuality. Individuality rests on inadequacy. And inadequate ideas are not illusory but real. But there is, Spinoza says, nothing positive in virtue of which inadequate ideas are false. Insofar as their content is "positive" they are, it seems, adequate. What then is error? In becoming clearer about this we can hope also to get a firmer grasp on the apparently tenuous reality of individuals.

Error for Spinoza is always a matter of inadequacy of ideas, and he explains this in terms of two concepts—passivity and fragmentation or incompleteness. Adequacy and inadequacy of ideas are connected, through activity and passivity, to the adequacy and inadequacy of causes. Causes are, in Spinoza's sense, "adequate" when it is possible to perceive their effects clearly and distinctly through them. The effects of inadequate causes, in contrast, cannot be explained through them alone (IIIDef1). Insofar as our minds have adequate ideas, they necessarily act; and, insofar as they have inadequate ideas, they necessarily suffer. To say that we "act" is to say that something is done of which we are the adequate cause—something which follows from our nature in such a way that it can be clearly and distinctly understood through it. On the other hand, we "suffer" or are passive when something is done within us or follows from our nature of which we are not an adequate cause (IIIDef2). The activity or passivity of the mind as idea thus depends on whether what happens is intelligible through the mind and its subsidiary ideas. If what happens can be understood only by taking into account extraneous ideas, the mind is, in relation to that happening, not active but passive. So inadequate ideas are also incomplete ideas, lacking full intelligibility without reference to other ideas in the wider context of the mind of God.

It may well seem strange that to judge whether a mind is active or passive we must take into account ideas outside that mind, treating it as just one idea in relation to others. Earlier, in the *Treatise on the Emendation of the Intellect*, Spinoza offered a more literal treatment of the mind's incompleteness than the *Ethics* version. There he associates inadequacy with our not being "thinking things in ourselves," but only "parts of a thinking thing" encompassed in the divine intellect. "If it is—as it seems at first—of the nature of a thinking being to form true, or adequate, thoughts, it is certain that inadequate ideas arise in us only from the fact that we are a part of a thinking being, of which some thoughts wholly constitute our mind, while others do so only in part (G. II/28; C. 33)."

Here adequate ideas are those thoughts of a larger intellect that occur in their entirety in, or as, the human mind. Inadequate ideas are fragments of thoughts that are complete in that mind. In the *Ethics* the relations between inadequacy and incompleteness are more complex and only misleadingly captured by the jigsaw model that comes so readily for the earlier version. For a start, the jigsaw model does not capture Spinoza's emphasis on the activity incorporated into Spinoza's "ideas"—his refusal to think of them as mute pictures on a panel, there to be observed or assessed by an external act of judgment. Ideas involve of their very nature affirmation or negation (IIP49S2). Spinoza's own rejection of the metaphor of pictures on a panel makes it difficult to think of the parts of a jigsaw as a model for what he means by fragmentation and completeness. The incompleteness of an inadequate idea is not just a quantitative matter, as if what is incomplete in the human mind becomes complete in the mind of God just by the addition of more facts. The point would then be a trivial one—that an isolated idea cannot include all there is to know. But why should an idea of something less than the whole be thereby less completely true of its limited object?

(48)

What then is the "incompleteness" of an inadequate idea? Spinoza presents the distinction between adequacy and inadequacy as that between two ways in which an idea can be considered—in relation to the human mind and in relation to the mind of God. There is "nothing positive" in ideas on account of which they are called false (IIP33). All ideas are in God. There is, after all, nowhere else for them to be. And insofar as they are not only "in" God but "related" to him, they are true (IIP32). The distinction is an elusive one.[3] And so too is the contrasted relation of ideas to human minds. There are no inadequate or confused ideas, he says, "except insofar as they are related to the singular Mind of someone" (IIP36Dem). But what is this relation to a singular mind? It is of course not just their being present in an individual mind. For we do have some ideas that are adequate—those that are in God "in so far as he constitutes the essence of our Mind" (IIP34Dem). An acceptable interpretation of Spinoza's account of inadequacy as incompleteness must be true to the spirit of his rejection of the "passive picture" model of ideas, while yet giving content to the distinction between ideas as "in" God and as "related" to him. If we take seriously Spinoza's incorporation of the act of judging into the idea, rather than seeing it as an extraneous act performed on a "mute picture on a panel," we cannot treat the difference between adequacy and inadequacy as a difference in attitude toward a neutral, independently identifiable content. Nor, it seems, can we think of inadequacy as coming from a distorted, perspectival view that it would make sense for a self-respecting mind to transcend. For the mind is itself an inadequate idea.

The Cartesian picture of an autonomous will performing acts of judgment on a passive, independently identifiable content exerts a strong pull that makes it harder for us to grasp Spinoza's way of thinking of inadequacy. For it encourages us to think of inadequacy as

---

3. Henry Allison comments on the apparent emptiness of Spinoza's talk of ideas considered in relation to God in *Benedict de Spinoza: An Introduction*, rev. ed. (New Haven: Yale University Press, 1987), p. 105.

either a defect in content or as a defect in the mind's attitude to that content. But for Spinoza inadequacy cannot be located on either side of such an act-content distinction. What then can it be?

Spinoza insists that there is "nothing positive" in virtue of which false ideas are false. Falsity is nothing positive, but just the "privation of knowledge which inadequate, or mutilated and confused, ideas involve" (IIP35). If there were a positive feature in virtue of which ideas were false, it could not exist in the mind of God. For there all ideas are "true and adequate." But there is nowhere else for such a feature of ideas to be. So it cannot be that the mind discerns some feature of an idea in virtue of which it judges it to be adequate. However his pains to avoid treating falsity as a kind of reality seem to put Spinoza at risk of undermining the very reality of false ideas. It is no less difficult to see how his false ideas can be real than it is to see how he can allow the reality of individuals. But the two problems have similar solutions.

We can begin to see a way through the perplexities if we think through what is involved in an idea being grasped in relation to an individual mind rather than in relation to God. All ideas, whether adequate or inadequate, are in God. The difference is that adequate ideas involve understanding bodily modifications through "common notions"—understanding what they have in common—in ways that prescind from the particularity of the minds in which are located the most basic and direct states of awareness of the modifications of our bodies. Because the direct awareness of our bodies involves the awareness of other bodies too (IIP16), these ideas must be confused (IIP28). Adequate knowledge of bodies is in God "not insofar as he is considered to be affected with the human Mind, but insofar as he is considered to be affected with other ideas (IIP28Dem)." It is not available from the perspective of my mind. Indeed it is misleading to think in terms of my mind having a perspective on my body—as if it were able to perceive my body in relation to other bodies from a position outside them all. The idea that constitutes the nature of a human mind is not, considered in itself alone, clear and distinct. And the same goes for the idea of that mind and the ideas of the ideas of the human body's affection, insofar as they are referred to the mind alone. "Anyone can easily see this" (IIP28S). The alleged clarity of the point may well be an exaggeration. But the upshot of these obscure but intriguing passages in Part Two of the *Ethics* seems to be that an idea, considered in relation to an individual mind rather than in relation to God, just is the direct awareness of body involved in sensation and imagination—the awareness that constitutes, at its most basic level, the mind as idea of body.

What of the other side of the distinction—the understanding of ideas of body in relation to God? Ideas thus understood, Spinoza insists, must be adequate and true. Are they the same ideas, considered now in a different set of relations, as those that are, in relation to an individual mind, inadequate? In a sense, yes. For they too are ideas of body, but grasped now in relation to other ideas of body and hence understood through "common notions." The body of which my mind is the direct, inadequate awareness can also be adequately understood in relation to other bodies. Indeed some of my own ideas of it can be adequate. But, again, we must be careful not to think of the contrast in terms of a single, independently identifiable item considered, on the one hand, in relation to the individual mind and, on the other, in relation to God. An inadequate idea does not exist at all except in relation to the individual mind. Individuality and inadequacy are interconnected. But inadequacy is no less real than the individuality of minds on which it depends. In fact Spinoza insists that inadequate and confused ideas "follow with the same necessity" as adequate, or clear and distinct ones (IIP36). It is at first sight a puzzling claim. There is a clear sense in which adequate ideas can be said to necessarily "follow" from one another. They are the kinds of mental item that it comes naturally to us to think of as standing in relations of entailment. But what is it for states of sensory awareness or of imagination to "follow necessarily"?

There are two ways of taking this, and they are in tension with one another, although each captures something important in Spinoza's treatment of inadequacy. On the one hand, we can say that inadequate ideas "follow with the same necessity" as adequate ones, just because, insofar as they can be said to "follow" at all, they cannot be distinguished from their "adequate" counterparts. We relate our inadequate ideas to God by understanding them in accordance with common notions. But, when we have done so, what is understandable in them "follows with the same necessity" as adequate ideas; for it is only the adequate ideas of reason—the ideas "common to all" and grasped equally in the whole and in the part—that can be said to "follow" at all. However Spinoza, in explicating his claim that inadequate ideas follow with the same necessity as adequate ones, refers us back to an earlier section of the text where he invokes what seems a very different kind of following. The "formal being" of things that are not modes of thinking, he says, does not follow from the divine nature because God has first known the things. Rather the objects of ideas follow and are inferred from their attributes "in the same way and by the same necessity" as that with which ideas follow from the attribute of thought (IIP6C).

Whereas Leibniz's God makes real possible individuals that he first knows—as Spinoza would put it—Spinoza's God is expressed with the same necessity, under both attributes. Ideas have no primacy over their objects. The shared "way" and "necessity" in which inadequate ideas follow is the same as those in which even material modes can be said to follow. There is much that is obscure—both about this following and necessity said to be common to adequate ideas, inadequate ideas, and material modes—and about how the fact that inadequate ideas exist only in relation to an individual mind is supposed to ground it. But it does bring home how far Spinoza is from seeing either individuality or inadequacy as an illusion to be shed by a mind bent on the cultivation of reason. The first way of interpreting the necessary "following" of inadequate ideas answers to Spinoza's rationalism. The second answers to his realistic recognition of the limitations of reason. It is a tension that runs right through the *Ethics*.

There is another aspect of Spinoza's treatment of adequate ideas that may seem to threaten, at another level, the coherence of his treatment of adequacy and inadequacy. The problem is to see how Spinoza can distinguish between different adequate ideas. Individuals, though real, exist only in relation to a finite mind. And, likewise, ideas are inadequate only in relation to a finite mind. Since these two relations of dependence are interconnected, it is not surprising that there should be an analogue here of the problem we have already seen in relation to Spinoza's treatment of individuals. It can appear at first sight that Spinoza must collapse all adequate ideas into the one all-encompassing totality in which inadequacy vanishes, just as it appeared that he must collapse individuals into the one Substance.

One ingenious solution has been offered by Thomas Mark.[4] Although the idea of each finite thing includes ideas of all others, each, he suggests, is a unique permutation of ideas in the mind of God. Adequate ideas of different individuals are differentiated through, as it were, a difference of focus. In an adequate idea of *x*, *x* is regarded as an effect and all other things as causes. The idea of *x* is the only idea in which *x* figures solely as an effect or logical consequence. But the difficulty for this resolution of the problem is to see how to explain such a difference of focus. What could give rise to the point of view from which one thing could be singled out as effect in relation to others as causes? The problem is to understand the shifts of attention that, for Mark, distinguish one adequate idea from another. Different perspectives seem to demand different perceiving minds. But to treat a mind as source of the perspective is difficult to reconcile with the mind

4. Thomas Mark, "Truth and Adequacy in Spinozistic Ideas," in Robert W. Shahan and John I. Biro, eds., *Spinoza: New Perspectives* (Norman: University of Oklahoma Press, 1978), pp. 11–34. The relations between truth and adequacy are further discussed in Mark's *Spinoza's Theory of Truth* (New York: Columbia University Press, 1972).

being itself an inadequate idea. Spinozistic perspectives are in this respect, as we have already seen, very different from those of a Cartesian ego, whose distorted view of reality can be attributed to its being mixed in with body. Minds are for Spinoza themselves part of the totality—ideas, and inadequate ones at that. They have no independence as intellectual substances that could ground the differentiation of ideas. Nor can the required shifts of focus be supplied by the mind of God. A shift of attention would have to be a specific mode of thought. And all such modes Spinoza relegates to the totality of *Natura Naturata*—Substance as expressed in the totality of modes (1P31 and Dem). Spinoza's God cannot focus his intellectual attention from outside the totality of modes of thought.

The role of perspectival awareness in Spinoza's account of the individuality of minds is in fact more radical than Mark's interpretation suggests. What provides the differentiation within the totality is the different sensory starting points from which the common notions are reached. As different selves, we are aware of different starting points, and this is what allows us to be differentiated within the totality. We do attain to common notions. But Spinoza's 'good' universals are not Cartesian clear and distinct ideas, pertaining to the structure of the mind as a purely intellectual and hence perspective-free observer. We arrive at the same common notions whatever the states of direct awareness from which we start. Even if we think of what is "necessary" in any inadequate ideas as what they have in common, what differentiates them from one another is the different points from which the transitions to common notions began. Since we are as minds direct awarenesses of body, our understanding begins within the totality. Our common notions are anchored in our status as ideas of particular bodies—unavoidable perspectives from which we perceive, confusedly, the whole. Although we form common notions, we cannot entirely transcend perceiving in relation to a particular mind. For such perspectival awareness constitutes our very existence as minds. Our inadequacy, no less than our individuality, is no illusion but our very reality. Let us now see how all this affects the Cartesian ideal of indubitable knowledge.

Skepticism

The contrasts between Descartes's and Spinoza's treatment of the relations between mind and body ground different theories of knowledge, with very different stances on issues of certainty and skeptical doubt. Descartes takes skepticism seriously. For him certainty is grounded in the overcoming of skeptical doubt—the reasoned repudiation of the possibility that thought might go its own way, detached from the external world it purports to mirror. For Spinoza there is no such possibility of a mismatch between the "order and connection" of ideas and that of things. Skeptical doubt is not a profound threat to the capacity for knowledge, to be allayed by reference to a reasoned proof of the existence of a benevolent God. It is rather a piece of nonsense resulting from a misunderstanding of mind's relations to body.

Cartesian knowledge is encapsulated in a "method" for moving from doubt to certainty—a method that emphasizes the observance of criteria for truth. For Spinoza, in contrast, there can be no criteria for truth—not because the skeptic's doubt cannot be repudiated, but because it should never have been taken seriously in the first place. Certainty just is the having of true ideas, and "method" is the reflective awareness of them. In the version of this idea of method elaborated in the *Treatise on the Emendation of the Intellect*, the mind starts from acts of knowledge and proceeds through reflection to an ever-increasing awareness of true ideas. Such a method, as Koyré points out in his introduction to the French translation of the work,[5] is of value only to a mind already assured of its possession of truth. Where Descartes's method is presented as a way of moving from error to truth, Spinoza

5. Alexandre Koyré, ed., *Traité de la reforme de l'entendement* (Paris: Vrin, 1974).

presents his own method as a reflection on knowledge already acquired, or on the process of its acquisition.

Spinoza elaborates the point through an analogy with the making of tools. In order to work iron, a hammer is needed. But that demands another hammer and other tools, and so on to infinity. But from all this it does not follow that human beings have no power to work iron. They at first used instruments supplied by nature to accomplish easy pieces of workmanship. "In the same way the intellect, by its inborn power, makes intellectual tools for itself, by which it acquires other powers for other intellectual works, and from these works still other tools, or the power of searching further, and so proceeds by stages, until it reaches the pinnacle of wisdom" (sec. 31; G. II/14; C. 17). Method must start from within knowledge. Rather than setting itself to acquire true ideas, it begins from the awareness of true ideas we already have. It follows, Spinoza thinks, that the skeptics should not be taken seriously. They are men whose minds are completely blinded, lacking consciousness of themselves (sec. 47; G. II/18; C. 22). They have not begun the process of reflection on knowledge already possessed, which is the path to self-knowledge and wisdom.

Method, thus construed as reflective knowledge, is at the same time self-knowledge, in a direct way that was not open to Descartes. For Descartes, as we have seen, the self was a separate object of knowledge, existing in a state of insulation from the world while containing innate representations of that world. The Cartesian self is transparent to itself. What is at issue is not its capacity to know itself but whether it can know anything else. And it is this epistemological gap between self-knowledge and knowledge of the rest of the world that made skepticism possible. For Spinoza, in contrast, the self is not at all the primary object of knowledge. Self-knowledge becomes a reflective dimension on our knowledge of the world—a world whose existence is never in doubt. Knowledge begins as immediate awareness of substance under the attribute of extension. This awareness is then progressively refined, issuing in self-awareness—a reflective form of the awareness of body.

Spinoza's brusque dismissals of skepticism, with his reiterations of the claim that there are no marks of truth—that truth is "its own standard"—may seem arbitrary and dogmatic. But the stance is grounded in his treatment of the relations between mind and body. The impossibility of skeptical doubt arises from the relation of identity between ideas and their objects and between ideas and the ideas of those ideas. The idea of the body and the body, that is, the mind and the body, are "one and the same Individual, which is conceived now under the attribute of Thought, now under the attribute of Extension." So the idea of the mind and the mind itself are "one and the same thing, which is conceived under one and the same attribute, viz. Thought" (11P21S). Spinoza sees these identities as involving the impossibility of skeptical doubt. The person who knows something thereby knows that he knows it, and that he knows that he knows that he knows, and so on to infinity. For every idea of body there is an idea of that idea, reflected into an infinite series of ideas. Any piece of knowledge, if we reflect on it at all, must be reflected in knowledge that we know. The uneasy Cartesian relation between mental representations and a material world that supposedly produces them is replaced by a confident reflection on knowledge already possessed—no more an object of possible doubt than the hammer that we refine through working on it with another hammer.

To think that we can have a true idea without knowing that we do is, Spinoza insists, again to suppose, as Descartes did, that an idea is something mute, like a picture on a tablet, rather than an active affirmation (11P43S). Why, we may ask, should we be any less likely to be deluded in actively affirming something than in thinking that a picture on a tablet corresponds to something? But this would be to misunderstand Spinoza's point. We can think we know something when in fact we do not. But assenting to something false, without doubting it, is for Spinoza not certainty (11P49S1). Certitude is not the "privation of doubt"—not just a lack of wavering of the imagination. It is in fact not to be construed as a psychological state at all. It is the act of understanding itself, considered in a way that prescinds from its relation to its object. Falsity is to be understood as the lack of certainty, construed in this way as a lack of activity in the mind. We can think we know something when in fact we do not. For Spinoza this is just a lack of wavering. What he denies is that we can have a true idea and yet doubt. Falsity can occur in the absence of doubt. But in a reflective mind truth cannot occur in the absence of certainty. For true certainty is just reflection on true ideas.

All this may seem a merely verbal dissolution of the problem of skepticism. But what Spinoza is resisting is the transition—implicit in Descartes's treatment of skepticism—from the possibility of having false ideas without doubting them to the possibility of doubting ideas that are in fact true. We can fail to doubt the false. But we cannot have a true idea without an affirmation. Any resistance we may feel to this central theme in his treatment of knowledge arises, he insists, from a reluctance to give up thinking of ideas as like images, for which correspondence to their objects is an extraneous property. To have an idea is to affirm something real. Knowledge does not, as Descartes suggested, begin from a mental replica, whose "marks of truth" justify our concluding that it does indeed correspond to something. Rather, we start from an affirmation of the real and refine our judgments through coming to a better understanding of what that involves, thereby increasing our self-awareness.

For Spinoza it is axiomatic that a true idea must agree with its object (1A6). Descartes would accept that there must be this agreement. But for him the agreement between idea and object rests on the veracity of God, who would not allow properly functioning thought to get out of alignment with matter. Descartes took seriously the possibility that our ideas might be all that ideas should be and yet have no external correlate. Spinoza rearranges the pieces in such a way that this possibility cannot be envisaged. A well-formed idea cannot lack its object, for idea and object are not separate items to be brought into alignment. They are one and the same thing—their identity grounded in that of thought and matter as different attributes of one substance. We cannot, then, stand in need of a proof, of the kind Descartes must supply, to establish that our adequate ideas are true.

Addressing himself to the question how we can know we have an idea that agrees with that of which it is the idea, Spinoza insists that he has shown "more than sufficiently" that he knows it just from having the true idea. "What can there be which is clearer and more certain than a true idea, to serve as a standard of truth? As the light makes both itself and the darkness plain, so truth is the standard both of itself and of the false" (IIP43S). So there is for Spinoza no room for doubt of the kind Descartes took so seriously about the existence of the world. Nor is there any suggestion that the wise mind should withdraw from matter to contemplate its own contents. The problem of skepticism— as the problem of what ideas, if any, our minds should affirm— disappears. There is no gap between ideas and reality within which skepticism might take up its questioning stance. What remains of skepticism, as we shall now see, is the tranquillity that the ancient skeptics thought would ensue from suspending judgment.

Judgment, Intellect, and Will

Spinoza argued against Descartes that ideas, insofar as they are ideas, carry affirmation with them, that the mind cannot suspend judgment by an act of will and, more generally, that there is in the mind no free will.[6] What has attracted most attention about these passages following IIP49 is their bearing on epistemological issues— on the avoidance of error, the requirements of certainty, the proper

6. A version of this section has been published under the title "Spinoza on the Distinction between Intellect and Will," in Edwin Curley and Pierre-François Moreau, eds., *Spinoza: Issues and Directions* (Leiden: Brill, 1990), pp. 113–24.

exercise of the mind in knowledge. Questions about the justification of claims to knowledge have of course loomed large in the philosophical tradition since Kant. And it is true that Spinoza is here attempting to undermine the Cartesian version of certainty and of the nature of error. But he does not offer an alternative way of moving from error to truth. And there is in any case more at stake here between Spinoza and Descartes than the epistemological debate that is salient from a post-Kantian perspective. In rejecting the will and insisting that the sole power of the mind resides in understanding, Spinoza assigns judgment to the realm of necessity, over which we have no control. For Descartes, in contrast, there was an element in judgment which did lie under human control, and this was the mark of human exemption from the realm of necessity. For both of them the consequences go beyond issues in the theory of knowledge.

Spinoza's treatment of the distinction between intellect and will points forward in the text to his version—a very different one from Descartes's—of reason's power over the passions. And it also points back to his treatment—again a very different one from Descartes's—of the contrasts between the human mind and the divine will and intellect. If we attend to its location in the text, we get a rather different perspective on the treatment of judgment from the one usually offered. Descartes and Spinoza take up different stances on issues that go back to the moral concerns of the ancient skeptics, no less than on issues discussed in more recent epistemology.

Descartes was of course concerned to secure the foundations of scientific knowledge against skeptical doubt. But, in recommending that we suspend judgment where we lack clear and distinct perception, he appropriated to the search for certainty some more skeptical concerns—about the right attitude to necessity, about whether we can control our destiny, about how to attain tranquillity and reconcile ourselves to mortality. Spinoza's responses to Descartes's treatment of the suspension of judgment are framed with a shared concern with such issues. The repudiation of the will's supposed role in judgment, he thinks, will tranquillize our spirits and show us our highest happiness and virtue. It is on these more ethical dimensions of their concern with skepticism that I wish to focus here.

Descartes's linking of judgment and volition, as Jonathan Bennett remarks with some puzzlement in *A Study of Spinoza's "Ethics,"*[7] cuts across the traditional distinction between cognitive and conative states. Philosophers traditionally distinguish cognition—knowledge, belief, understanding—from conation—disliking, wanting, intending, trying. Descartes in contrast, as Bennett points out, puts sensing, imagining, and abstract thought into one category; disliking, affirming, and denying into another. In repudiating the role of the will in judgment, Spinoza does not reaffirm the traditional dichotomy between the cognitive and the conative. Rather, in identifying will and understanding, he transforms the concept of understanding so that it becomes conative. And he does this, here as in other parts of the *Ethics,* by pushing further points that Descartes had already stressed.

For Descartes the capacity to choose is the essence of the will; and this capacity is manifested in the liberty to abstain from judgment, from giving or withholding assent, which we discover in ourselves through enacting the method of doubt. This capacity, he says in the *Principles,* is the greatest human perfection (Part I, sec. 37; AT VIIIA, 19; Cott. I, 205); and, in the *Passions of the Soul,* he presents it as making the human mind God-like (Part III, art. 152; AT XI, 445; Cott. I, 384). In the Fourth Meditation he suggests that in fact the human will, considered in itself, is of no less stature than the divine will, the superiority of which arises solely from the greater knowledge and power conjoined with it. The combination of the infinite, active faculty of will with the finite, passive faculty of understanding is the source of our errors; and we avoid error by schooling the will to assent only in the presence of ideas that are clear and distinct.

7. Jonathan Bennett, *A Study of Spinoza's "Ethics"* (Cambridge: Cambridge University Press, 1984), p. 159.

But there are for Descartes restraints on this power of autonomous choice; and Spinoza exploits them to collapse the Cartesian distinction between will and intellect into his own doctrine that the power of the mind resides in understanding only—an understanding that is itself subject to the necessities that govern the rest of nature. In the lack of accompanying will, however, understanding does not remain a bare cognitive state. It becomes conative, though not in a way that could be summed up in Descartes's idea of the will as wishing or shunning, seeking or avoiding. The essence of Spinoza's conative understanding becomes not choice but acquiescence. And this is at the center of his differences with Descartes.

For Descartes the freedom of the will is inconsistent with subjection to external causes. It is manifested in the fact that, in affirming or denying, seeking or avoiding what is placed before us by the understanding, we act without being conscious that any outside force constrains us. But clear and distinct ideas, as well as God's grace, determine the will without interfering with its freedom as "external" causes would. To be free, he says in the Fourth Meditation, and in Part One of the *Principles,* it is not necessary to be indifferent as to the choice between two contraries. The indifference we feel when we are not swayed to one side by reason is in fact the lowest grade of liberty, showing a lack in knowledge rather than a perfection of will. If we always recognized clearly what was true or good, we should have no trouble in deliberating as to what judgment or choice we should make but be entirely free without ever being indifferent. The most striking illustration of this absence of indifference is of course Descartes's certainty of his own existence. He cannot prevent himself from believing that a thing so clearly conceived is true—not because he finds himself compelled to do so by some external cause, but simply because from great clearness in his mind there follows a great inclination of his will. He believes in his own existence, he says, with so much greater freedom or spontaneity as he possesses the less indifference toward it. In relation to other matters, and especially in relation to matter, the will lacks a compelling reason to assent; and the appropriate course is to withhold judgment. If he abstains from assenting when he does not perceive with sufficient clearness and distinctness, he acts rightly. But if he determines to deny or affirm, he no longer uses his free will as he should.

On this picture, Spinoza performs a devastatingly simple conceptual maneuver. The belief in the will, grounded for Descartes in the lack of knowledge of external causes, becomes for Spinoza just that lack—ignorance of the external causes that govern our minds and their operations, along with the rest of nature. In the mind there is, he says, no free will, but the mind is determined to wish this or that by a cause, which has also been determined by another cause, and so on to infinity (IIp48). Even more ingenious, though to us rather less accessible, is the way Spinoza exploits Descartes's other crucial point—that the highest grade of freedom is the mind's 'free' assent in the presence of clear and distinct perception. And he exploits it by following through the implications of what for Descartes was the antithesis of freedom in the mind—the mind's inclusion in a totality of finite causes.

The thought that human minds and their ideas should be, along with everything else, determined by external causes does not easily coexist with our sense of freedom—imbued as we are with the spirit of Descartes's, and later Kant's, commitment to the autonomous rational will. But for Spinoza the mind's subjection to external causes follows from the claim, which Descartes would have had difficulty rejecting, that strictly God is the only "free cause," able to act solely by the laws of his own nature (IP17C2). And it is a further consequence of God's being the only free cause that our minds and their ideas are included in a totality of thought, in which truth is affirmed freely, though necessarily, in a way that echoes and incorporates Descartes's "highest grade of liberty." The mind's subjection to external causes is rendered harmless by being accommodated into the "mind of God" which affirms the material universe. Spinoza's account of human judgment is framed by his treatment of the human mind as part of the infinite intellect of

God. And that in turn is related to his discussion of divine will and understanding in Part One. But before turning to that, I want to look briefly at what Descartes had to say about the will of God.

For Descartes our capacity to suspend judgment manifests the separation of human will and intellect, whereas in God's case they are inseparable. Having senses, he says in the *Principles,* involves passivity, which indicates dependence. Hence it cannot be supposed that God has senses, but only that he understands and wills. "And even his understanding and willing does not happen, as in our case, by means of operations that are in a certain sense distinct one from another; we must rather suppose that there is always a single identical and perfectly simple act by means of which he simultaneously understands, wills, and accomplishes everything" (Part 1, sec. 23; AT viiiA, 13; Cott. 1, 201). The unity of divine intellect and will, as Descartes himself saw, suggests that everything happens of necessity, that God makes real everything of which he can form the idea, so that all things possible must come to be. But, as Leibniz later complained, Descartes drew back from the full consequences of that idea, which were made explicit by Spinoza.[8] One of the restraints for Descartes here was of course the freedom of the human will, in which we resemble God. If our wills are free, their results must remain indeterminate, although we cannot comprehend, he says in the *Principles,* how God leaves them indeterminate. In a familiar Cartesian move in response to the appearance of contradiction, he urges us not to try to think both free will and God's preordaining at the same time (Part 1, sec. 40; AT viiiA, 20; Cott. 1, 206).

Descartes hankers strongly after necessities, although that conflicts with his other strong conviction—the freedom of the human will. His version of the mind's tranquillity is poised uneasily between the acceptance of necessity and the self-esteem that comes from our sense of

8. Leibniz, letter to Philipp, end of January 1680; Gerhardt, 4, 283–84; in Leroy E. Loemker, trans. and ed., *Leibniz: Philosophical Papers and Letters,* 2d ed. (Dordrecht: Reidel, 1969), p. 273.

control over our lives. In the *Passions of the Soul* he speaks of the folly of vain desires, of wanting to change the things that cannot be changed. The remedy lies in schooling our desires to accord with true judgments, the proper arms of the soul. Desire is always good when it conforms to true knowledge and cannot fail to be bad when it is founded on error. When we err in relation to desire it is because we do not sufficiently distinguish the things that depend entirely on us from those that do not so depend. Things that depend on us alone, that is on our own free will, cannot be too ardently desired, and we should always receive from them all the satisfaction we expected (Part II, sec. 144; AT XI, 437; Cott. I, 379).

For Descartes then we avoid vain desire through self-reliance, by retreating to what depends on us alone. All that lies beyond our control should be assigned to the inscrutable wisdom of providence. In a passage that seems to anticipate Spinoza, Descartes urges us to reflect that it is impossible that anything should happen in any other way than as it has been determined by providence from all eternity. The appearance that things happen by chance is founded only on the fact that we do not know all the causes that contribute to each effect (Part II, sec. 145; AT XI, 438; Cott. I, 380). The eternal decree of providence is so infallible and immutable that, apart from the things it has willed to leave dependent on our own free will, nothing happens to us that is not necessary and "as it were by fate," so that we should not desire that it happen otherwise. But because most of our desires extend to things that do not depend entirely on us, nor entirely on others, we ought to distinguish in them what does depend only on us, in order to limit our desire to that alone (Part II, sec. 146; AT XI, 439; Cott. I, 380).

Descartes's concept of the will amounts to this idea of what depends only on us. The will is the mind's principal activity, in which it exerts its freedom, expresses its autonomous selfhood. Yet what happens, he also thinks, is absolutely decreed by fate and immutable. We should nonetheless endeavor to choose by reason, not because we can have any confidence that it will affect the outcome, but because it strengthens and cultivates the "internal emotions" that the soul excites in itself. Following after virtue does not ensure a good outcome, as far as external events are concerned. The area of what depends only on us, it emerges, is really an inward zone of contentment. None of the troubles that come from elsewhere have any power to harm the soul. They serve rather to increase its joy, for in seeing that it cannot be harmed by them the soul is more sensible of its perfection. "And in order that our soul should have the means of happiness, it needs only to pursue virtue diligently. For if anyone lives in such a way that his conscience cannot reproach him for ever failing to do something he judges to be the best (which is what I here call 'pursuing virtue') he will receive from this a satisfaction which has such power to make him happy that the most violent assaults of the passions will never have sufficient power to disturb the tranquillity of his soul" (*Passions of the Soul,* Part II, sec. 148; AT XI, 442; Cott. I, 382).

To follow after virtue is to exercise the will aright. We can then rest content in our self-esteem, secure in the knowledge that the onslaught of external causes has no power to harm our true selves. We will see in the next chapter how Descartes develops this in his treatment of reason's control over the passions. What is important here is that, in recommending that we suspend judgment in the lack of clear and distinct perception, Descartes accommodates judgment into this general account of following after virtue. Such judgments belong in the domain of what lies within our control. So human judgment escapes the dreaded state of subjection to external causes. Either it is elicited from us in a spontaneous and in the highest sense 'free' response to clear and distinct perception, or, where it is lacking, it remains under the control of a free will, in the exercise of which we rightly esteem ourselves as superior to the rest of nature. This then is the ethical dimension of Descartes's redrawing of the boundaries between the cognitive and the conative. We avoid error through a virtuous exercise of free will. The practice of Cartesian method becomes an occasion for moral self-esteem, an expression of our superiority over the rest of nature, bound as it is by necessity. The foundations of knowledge are thus secured through an exercise of virtue.

Such is the ethical rationale of Descartes's account of judgment. The Spinozistic picture is of course very different. For Spinoza there is no providence. God acts solely by the laws of his own nature, without ends or purposes. He acts, as Spinoza says at IIP3S, by the same necessity as that by which he understands himself. All that can be thought must be. It is a stronger version of the unity of divine intellect and will than Descartes ambivalently affirmed. There is no area of indeterminacy in which the human will might affect the course of events. That God acts by necessity means too that any sense of intellect or will that would apply to him can provide no model for a human will, no respect in which we might find our minds to be God-like. The divine mind, precisely because it does produce everything that is thinkable, must be as different from ours, in respect of both intellect and will, as the dog in the heavens from the dog that barks—a resemblance in name only (IP17S).

Those who have asserted that God's intellect, God's will, and God's power are one and the same, Spinoza suggests, have dimly grasped this truth. What is means is that the concept of will is subsumed into the idea of an understanding which is of its nature productive. Intellect, in any sense in which it could be applied to God, could not be, as our intellect is generally thought to be, "posterior to or simultaneous with" the things understood. God, by reason of his status as "free cause," is prior to all things. Whereas our intellect follows the truth, God's intellect precedes it. The truth is as it is because it exists objectively in the intellect of God. The relations of priority and posteriority here are of course not meant to be temporal ones. The point is that, whereas our intellects must match themselves to an independent truth, the truth depends on God's intellect. And, given the kind of relationship that holds between Spinozistic attributes— each expressing completely all that can be—whatever material modes exist do not exist because God has had representations of them in thought.

Spinoza's God, unlike the God of Leibniz, does not make things to accord with exemplars inhabiting his understanding, awaiting the exercise of creative will. Whatever is thinkable exists, but not because it has first been thought. "The formal being of things which are not modes of thinking does not follow from the divine nature because [God] has first known the things; rather the objects of ideas follow and are inferred from their attributes in the same way and by the same necessity as that with which we have shown ideas to follow from the attribute of Thought" (11P6C). God's power of thinking is equal to his realized power of action. So "whatever follows formally from God's infinite nature follows objectively in God from his idea in the same order and with the same connection" (11P7C). All this is a consequence of Spinoza's version of substance: "The thinking substance and the extended substance are one and the same substance, which is now comprehended under this attribute, now under that"—a truth that was seen "as if through a cloud," by some of the Hebrews, when they maintained that "God, God's intellect, and the things understood by him are one and the same" (11P7S).

Spinoza's insistence on the utter causal independence of the unfolding of the corresponding attributes sometimes seems to bring him to the point of contradiction. Thus in the second Scholium to 1P17 he elaborates on the claim that God's intellect is neither posterior nor simultaneous to the things understood by saying that "the truth and formal essence of things is what it is because it exists objectively in that way in God's intellect." But is not that to suggest that the truth of a material thing's existence—and hence its existence—is as it is *because* of an idea existing "objectively" in God? However, the "because" here is not meant to express a causal relation across attributes. The "truth and formal essence of things"—even where the truth concerns matter—is located under the attribute of thought. The truth of God's idea of the existence of a material mode does not make it exist any more than the truth of snow's whiteness causally produces white snow.

So much for the divine intellect and will. What bearing does all that have on Spinoza's distinction between human will and intellect in Part Two? Our intellect and will, as he has stressed in Part One, must be utterly different in kind from any sense of intellect or will that could be applied to substance. We cannot look to the divine intellect or will to provide a model for our own. But our minds, though utterly different in kind from God conceived as free cause—as *Natura Naturans*—are nonetheless part of the mind of God that is the realization of the total power of substance under the attribute of thought. Wherever we are dealing with a mode of thought, it has to be referred not to *Natura Naturans* but to *Natura Naturata* (1P31). The mind of God, of which our minds are part, is the totality of all that follows, under the attribute of thought, from the power of substance. We are not part of the "dog in the heavens" intellect, but of the "dog that barks" version. But, with that proviso, we are indeed part of the infinite intellect of God. When we say that the human mind perceives something, what that really means is that God has the idea, although, if the idea is adequately understood only in conjunction with other ideas outside the mind, the human mind perceives it only inadequately (11P11C). Spinoza himself acknowledges, as we have seen, that this encompassing of the human mind and its subsidiary ideas in the infinite intellect of God can be expected to bring his readers to a halt in comprehension—a mind-stopping suspension of judgment, as Descartes would have it. But if we do, as Spinoza urges, persist a little with this strange but tantalizing suggestion and try to see it in the context of his earlier discussion of the concepts of intellect and will, we get some insight into what is going on in his repudiation of Cartesian will.

Let us turn now to those notoriously inadequate considerations that Spinoza advances, in the passages following 11P49, to justify his rejection of the Cartesian distinction between human will and intellect. There is in the mind, he says, no affirmation and negation save that which an idea, inasmuch as it is an idea, involves. The mind's affirmation involves the idea that is affirmed; and, less obviously, the idea involves the affirmation. Spinoza gets to this conclusion by taking what seems an unreasonably favorable case: the affirmation that a triangle involves angles equal to two right angles. This idea of a triangle, he says, can neither be nor be conceived without the affirmation. Therefore the affirmation belongs to the essence of the idea of a triangle and is nothing besides. What we have said of this volition, he continues, "inasmuch as we have selected it at random," may be said of any other volition, namely that it is nothing but an idea. The obvious rejoinder, of course, is that the example has not been taken at random. The flow-on from idea to affirmation, which does hold here, does not apply to what we would see as nonnecessary truths. It is certainly true that Spinoza has not chosen his example at random. But he has not chosen it merely out of a desire to trade on the peculiar features of a favorable case. It is an example that he used in Part One to illustrate the point that all things flow of necessity from the power of God. "From God's supreme power, or infinite nature, infinitely many things in infinitely many modes, i.e., all things, have necessarily flowed, or always follow, by the same necessity and in the same way as from the nature of a triangle it follows, from eternity and to eternity, that its three angles are equal to two right angles. So God's omnipotence has been actual from eternity and will remain in the same actuality to eternity. And in this way, at least in my opinion, God's omnipotence is maintained far more perfectly" (1P17S1).

From the perspective of an individual human mind, there is of course a world of difference between the idea of the triangle, in relation to the sum of its angles, and contingent truths in relation to their subjects. But for Spinoza this distinction holds precisely because of the limited position held by an individual mind as part of the totality of thought. The necessity of the truth about the triangle rests on "common notions," which are equally present in the part and in the whole and hence not subject to the error that results from our fragmentary awareness. About triangles, it is possible to have adequate knowledge, even if for any one of us there is a great deal about their properties we do not know. That is to say, in Spinoza's terminology, the adequate idea of the triangle can occur in God insofar as he constitutes an individual human mind. But there are other ideas that are not adequate in our minds—ideas that are in God only insofar as he "also has the idea of another thing together with the human Mind" (IIPIIC).

There is for us a very real distinction between the kind of knowledge we can have of triangles and our knowledge of contingent truths. Spinoza does not wish to deny that distinction. What he does want to say is that the distinction drops out within the total context of all the ideas in the mind of God. In relation to the totality of thought, there is for Spinoza no distinction of the kind Leibniz invokes between those truths that depend only on God's understanding and those that depend on his will. The belief in contingency in general, as in the particular case of belief in human free will, just amounts to our ignorance of causes. "In nature there is nothing contingent, but all things have been determined from the necessity of the divine nature to exist and produce an effect in a certain way" (IP29).

The adequacy that is lacking within the limits of a mind is supplied in wider contexts of which it is a part. To say that all things flow from God's nature with the same necessity as the sum of its angles flows from the nature of a triangle is to say that in the infinite intellect of God all truths are necessary. But their affirmation is not always encompassed in our minds. Ideas are always accompanied by affirmation, but the affirmation is not always "ours" in Descartes's sense. But is not this to admit that what in the intellect of God is affirmed is, in our mind, present without affirmation—that the idea that is affirmed in the mind of God is in our mind merely entertained? And is not this to admit that for the human mind, unlike the mind of God, we do after all need a distinction between will and intellect? But we can make that objection only if we detach the idea from the affirmation, which is precisely what Spinoza will not allow us to do. To continue the spatial metaphors, wherever an idea is, there the affirmation must be. To think that one and the same idea could be present, unaffirmed, in a human mind and, affirmed, in the mind of God is to think, again, in terms of the Cartesian picture—of ideas as laid out like mute pictures on a tablet, as Spinoza puts it, with the affirmation added from elsewhere.

Still, we may say, something must be able to be present, unaffirmed, in the human mind, or the whole problem would not arise. Spinoza's discussion of this in the illustration of the boy imagining a winged horse is not at first sight helpful in countering our Cartesian prejudices. Spinoza grants that the boy can imagine the horse without being in error, but denies that in the act of perception he does not make any affirmation. If the boy does have just the idea of the winged horse, he insists, then it is affirmed. "For what is perceiving a winged horse other than affirming wings of the horse?" (11P49S3, sec. B(ii)). His mind may be in error, but, again, that is not because of a misuse of free will, but just through the fragmentation involved in being part of a whole. We can explain the error, Spinoza thinks, without having to suppose that an idea lies unaffirmed in the mind. But what of the cases where the boy imagines the horse without affirming its existence, either because he judges correctly that it does not exist or because he does not judge one way or the other? Surely in those cases Spinoza must admit that there is in the mind an idea that is not affirmed? This is another of those points in the text where Spinoza's argumentation seems all too swift. What we want to see as an unaffirmed idea, he transforms into a different affirmed one—of the nonexistence of the horse or, at any rate, an affirmation of something inconsistent with its existence. And what we want to see as the presence in the mind of an idea in the lack of any propositional attitude, he transforms into a perception of inadequacy. Suspension of judgment, he says, is strictly speaking a perception and not an exercise of free will. When we say that someone suspends his judgment, we merely mean that he sees that he does not perceive the matter in question adequately.

But surely we must be able to consider the original idea of the horse before we arrive at any of these outcomes? Spinoza's treatment of these cases is all too brief. But he means it to be taken in conjunction with a remark he makes in the preamble to his replies to the Cartesian position, where he warns of the need to have an accurate distinction between ideas, on the one hand, and words and images, on the other. An idea, being a mode of thinking, does not, he says, consist in the image of anything or in words. Words and images are constituted by bodily motions, that do not at all involve the concept of thought (11P49S2). For Spinoza, images—which Descartes treated as confused ideas present in the mind through the causal influence of body—are not ideas at all. The boy's "image" of the horse, insofar as it does not involve affirmation, is not an idea either. That ideas are not images but modes of thinking means that they do not mediate between judgment and an external material reality. Judgment involves the affirmation of something real, not the affirmation that something real corresponds to a mental representation. There are layerings of ideas of ideas, super-imposed endlessly on the most fundamental level of knowledge. But Spinozistic ideas, to appropriate Wittgenstein's comment on language in the *Tractatus*, "reach right out to reality," articulating it, affirming it. What exactly is involved in this unmediated relationship between ideas and reality is by no means clear. But it is clear that the removal of the passive pictures involved in Cartesian judgment makes for a very different view of the act of judging.

Bennett, in his *Study of Spinoza's "Ethics,"* criticizes Spinoza's ac-count of judgment as involving the implausible claim that all ideas come before the mind as beliefs (pp. 162–67). But if we accept Spi-noza's account or judgment, we must see the "coming before the mind" locution as inappropriate. Spinoza is not saying that we believe compulsively whatever comes before the mind. That is mistaken in the same way as Leibniz's account of the implications of Spinoza's rejection of the distinction between divine will and intellect. Spinoza's God does not compulsively make real all the possibilities that occur to him. Rather, in the lack of a distinction between will and intellect, there is no array of possibles waiting to be made real. Leibniz's own treatment of the divine will choosing freely, but without indifference, the best, in the face of compelling reason, echoes Descartes's treatment of human judgment, choosing the truth. For Spinoza, in contrast, the human mind does not exert rational will in choosing the truth in the presence of compelling reason. And it is also misleading to present it as compulsively believing image-like ideas that come before it for judgment. The array of passive ideas awaiting the mind's choice disappears. Nor can it be said that beliefs come passively before the mind. It is true that the mind is aware of images. But they are bodily traces, affections of body—part of the totality of material modes which correspond to the totality of thought.

Where does all this leave skepticism? If everything happens as a necessary expression in thought or matter of the full power of substance, the supposed problem of skepticism—as an issue of which ideas our minds should affirm—disappears. What remains of skepticism is the tranquillity that the ancient skeptics thought would ensue from the suspension of judgment. But there is no suggestion that the existence of the world is open to doubt or that the wise mind should withdraw to contemplate its own contents. The infinite intellect of God, the total expression in thought of the power of substance, affirms in an intellectual love the corresponding order of material things, whose existence is not at issue. And the human mind participates in that, however inadequate and partial may be its understanding of its place in it.

Love, on Descartes's account of it in the *Passions of the Soul* (Part II, arts. 79, 80; AT XI, 387; Cott. I, 356), is the mind's voluntary uniting of itself with the loved object, an act of the will. For Spinoza the wish to unite with the loved object cannot be a free decision of the mind. For he has, he thinks, shown that to be fictitious. It becomes instead "a Satisfaction in the lover on account of the presence of the thing loved, by which the lover's Joy is strengthened or at least encouraged" (III Def. Aff. VI). Applied to the love of wisdom, the point becomes this: we do not, as Descartes thought, "choose the truth" as a free response to a compelling reason in the form of clear and distinct perception; nor do we follow virtue by training a faculty of will to withhold judgment where that compelling reason is lacking. Judgment is not a matter of wishing or avoiding. That is not to say it is compulsive. Nor is it to say it is a bare cognitive act, devoid of conative force. There is no choice here. But we do find a contentment in knowledge. In terms of Descartes's distinction, that contentment comes not from self-satisfaction in the right exercise of a god-like will, but from an affirmation of necessity. For Descartes, as we will see in more detail in the next chapter, the key to all the virtues and the remedy for the disorder of the passions is reflection on our free will (*Passions of the Soul*, Part III, arts. 152, 153; AT XI, 445–46; Cott. I, 384). For Spinoza, in the lack of the will, the remedial role shifts to intellect, now construed as an intellectual love, a conative understanding. The mind rests content in affirmation of and acquiescence in body, the awareness of which defines its being, although it knows its understanding of body is inevitably partial and confused.

All this amounts to a richer view of our intellectual lives than the disagreeable picture of our minds as compulsive yea-sayers, to which Bennett reduces Spinoza's account of judgment. But it involves of course a view of mind and world which is in many ways alien to us, influenced, as we are, by Cartesian theory of knowledge.

THREE

O

Reason and the Passions

Spinoza regarded it as something of a novelty that his philosophy treats human passions as just as fitting a subject as mathematics for rational investigation. The affects, he says in the preface to Part Three of the *Ethics*, should be treated in the geometric style, strange though it may seem to those philosophers who see human beings as disturbing, rather than following, the order of nature, that he should wish to treat in that way things which are contrary to reason. Human actions and appetites should be treated just as if their investigation were "a Question of lines, planes and bodies." Our passions are part of nature, not aberrations from it. Human impotence does not result from defects of human nature but from the common power of nature, of which we are part. Nothing happens in nature which can be attributed to any flaw in it, for the laws and rules according to which all things happen and change from one form to another are always and everywhere the same.

Novel though his approach to the passions may be, Spinoza acknowledges that he has a predecessor—the "celebrated Descartes." Although Descartes shared with those who saw the passions as aberrations the belief that the mind has absolute power over its own actions, he did nonetheless seek to explain human affects through their first causes. Like Spinoza, he based the mind's power over the affects in its understanding of them. His was a praiseworthy attempt to bring together freedom and understanding, but one, Spinoza ironically remarks, which showed in fact nothing but the cleverness of his understanding.

In the preface to Part Five, Spinoza's irony at Descartes's expense is heavier. Had Descartes's account of how we attain freedom from the passions not been so subtle, he says, he could hardly have believed it to have been propounded by so great a man. "Indeed, I cannot wonder enough that a Philosopher of his caliber—one who had firmly decided to deduce nothing except from principles known through themselves, and to affirm nothing which he did not perceive clearly and distinctly, one who had so often censured the Scholastics for wishing to explain obscure things by occult qualities—that such a Philosopher should assume a Hypothesis more occult than any occult quality."

From the perspective of Spinoza's own treatment of the passions, what Descartes has failed to do is to effectively bring together the understanding of the passions with our power over them. His own account integrates the scientific and the ethical concerns. It is in the act of understanding a passion that we become free of it. Let us look now at the features of Descartes's philosophy which make it difficult for him to achieve this Spinozistic synthesis and at the steps by which Spinoza transforms the Cartesian picture into his own. Three things are crucial, and they are interrelated: Descartes's notoriously sharp distinction between mind and body; his separation of the mind's practical concern with self-preservation—avoiding pain and pursuing pleasure—from his theoretical concerns; and his commitment to the will.

It is not surprising that Spinoza's charge of occultness should center on Descartes's attempt to explain the causal interaction of mind and body. On the one hand, he has distanced himself from the Aristotelian "substantial forms" that supposedly conditioned the behavior of distinct portions of matter. The appeal to mind-like principles, lurking in the physical world, is inconsistent with his sharp distinction between mind and matter. This exile of forms from the realm of matter opens up the possibility of a unitary account of the whole of nature. But Spinoza sees Descartes as abandoning his commitment to the unitariness of nature when he has to deal with the realm of intermingling of mind and matter—the realm of the passions of the soul, produced in mind by the movement of the animal spirits. And the intrusion of the will into matter, which is involved in Descartes's version of the remedy of the passions, further disrupts the unitariness of nature. Descartes is left with an incongruous causal transaction between things that have nothing in common. The will supposedly exerts a counterforce to the movement of the animal spirits—a mental event quaintly united with a "little portion of quantity." It is an occult hypothesis that defies Descartes's own demand for clear and distinct concepts. Faced with the challenge of including the relations between reason and passions in the scope of rational investigation, the celebrated Descartes abandons his own high standards of adequacy in explanation. Mind-body interaction cannot be accommodated into a schema whose very existence demands their rigid separation. Both the understanding of the passions and their remedy become casualties of Descartes's failure to resolve the tensions between mind-body separateness and their union in that Cartesian anomaly—an embodied human being.

Spinoza's own version of reason as remedy of the passions, although it may seem a radical departure from Descartes, can be seen as a restructuring of the Cartesian account—a retelling of the story that retains and renders more perspicuous many of Descartes's insights. Where Descartes emphasized the will, Spinoza defines the power of the mind by understanding only. So it must be understanding alone that contains the remedy of the passions. But he shows the superfluity of the Cartesian will precisely by pushing further than Descartes himself his insights into the nature of the passions.

Part of Nature

Descartes's 'Remedy': The Role of the Will

Despite Descartes's emphasis on the will in the *Passions of the Soul,* its direct role in controlling the passions is in fact quite limited. Although the will can directly control the movements of the pineal gland, exerting a counterforce to change the direction of the animal spirits, there is no question of our being able at will to redirect the course of the spirits in any way that would amount to control of the passions. In response to the turmoil of passion at full strength, the most the will can achieve is a holding operation. If fear incites our legs to flee, the will can usually restrain them. If anger causes us to lift a hand to strike, the will can usually hold it back. But for any sustained control of passion, the soul must resort to long-term strategies, taking up its proper weapons—firm and determinate judgments about good and evil (Part I, art. 48; AT XI, 367; Cott. I, 347).

The key to Descartes's remedy of the passions is not the will's direct power to resist, but rather the mind's capacity to detach itself from a present passion—retreating to a thought opposed to or at any rate independent of it. Detached from the immediacy of passion, the soul can then break the natural nexus that joins certain thoughts to certain motions of the spirits. In relation to the movement of his legs, the soldier comes to think not of safety but disgrace. The general remedy for the passions involves this "forethought and diligence" through which we can control our natural faults by striving to separate within ourselves the movement of the blood and spirits from the thoughts to which they are usually joined.

The will's power to directly control the movements of the pineal gland is soon overpowered by the effects of the movements of the spirits. But the soul's capacity to break up and re-form the natural connections between movements of the spirits and particular thoughts gives a more lasting power of resistance. The power of the will over passion is thus mediated through thought. It is the same power that makes human beings capable of language—equally, for Descartes, a disruption of 'natural' connections between bodily motions and representations (Part I, art. 50; AT XI, 369; Cott. I, 348).

This theme of detachment from the immediacy of passion—of a retreat to a realm of thought seen as the proper domain of selfhood—is central to Descartes's treatment of the passions. We see it in his discussion of the "internal emotions of the soul," as he calls them—emotions supposedly produced by the soul itself, in contrast to passions, which depend on some external movement of the spirits (Part II, art. 147; AT XI; Cott. I, 381). Although they can be accompanied by passions similar to them, they are also often at odds with the passions, and it is in this opposition that we best see their "internal" character. Descartes's examples are not altogether persuasive. A grieving husband feels a secret joy in his innermost soul, in opposition to the sadness aroused in him by the funeral display, the absence of a customary companion, and the remnants of love and pity, which draw tears from his eyes. His second example is of the pleasures of reading or the theater, intellectual joys that can originate from and coexist with the sadness inspired by the spectacle just as well as from other more joyful passions.

The examples are confusing. They seem to involve not one but several contrasts—between responses that do or do not depend on how others perceive us; between shared social responses as against those we feel individually; between responses to the here and now as against those that have been conditioned by past experience; between what we might now call "authentic" and "inauthentic" emotions. The widower's joy may come straight from his soul now. But it has been conditioned by past responses in a social world, which makes it no less dependent on body than his present public grief. But the point Descartes is making through the examples seems clear enough. There are joys of the soul that can be at odds with more "external" sadness. These joys provide a domain that is the soul's own, to which it may retreat from the afflictions of harmful, intrusive passion. The internal emotions, he says, "affect us more intimately, and consequently have much more power over us than the passions which occur with them but are distinct from them" (Part II, art. 148; AT XI, 442; Cott. I, 381–82). These internal emotions allow us to distance ourselves from the immediacy of passion, providing a stronger force of resistance than a blind will can achieve of its own resources. However, the most effective form of this detachment waits upon the formation of habits that are more securely integrated into the soul's structure than these episodic internal emotions. No amount of human wisdom is capable of counteracting the movement of the spirits when we are not adequately prepared, and few sufficiently prepare themselves for the contingencies of life by developing habits that will carry them through the times when their blood is "all in turmoil."

The most important of these habits of the soul is the one Descartes calls *générosité*—rightful self-esteem. In Part Three of the *Passions of the Soul*, as we have seen, he grounds rational self-esteem in the exercise of free will, which renders us in a certain way like God, by making us masters of ourselves (Part III, art. 152; AT XI, 445; Cott. I, 384). Developing the concept, he says that true *générosité* has two components. The first consists in our knowing that nothing truly belongs to us but the freedom to dispose of our volitions, and that we ought to be praised or blamed for no other reason than using our freedom well or badly. The second consists in our feeling within ourselves a firm and constant resolution to use our free will well—that is, never to lack the will to undertake and carry out whatever we judge to be best. To do this is to "pursue virtue in a perfect manner." All we should esteem in ourselves is a virtuous will (Part III, art. 153; AT XI, 446; Cott. I, 384).

Générosité is the key to all the virtues and a general remedy for every disorder of the passions, giving us complete control over them. Those with *générosité* have mastery over their desires, and over jealousy and envy, because whatever they think worth pursuing depends only on themselves; over hatred of others, because they esteem them as equally capable of a virtuous will; over fear, because of the self-assurance that their confidence in their own virtue gives them; and over anger, because they have very little esteem for everything that depends on others, and so they never give their enemies any advantage by acknowledging that they are injured by them (Part III, art. 156; AT XI, 448; Cott. I, 385). Rightful self-esteem protects us from dependence on what others think of us. But it also strengthens in us a healthier form of regard for others. The virtuous will, for which we rightly esteem ourselves, is equally attainable by others. "Those who possess this knowledge and this feeling about themselves readily come to believe that any other person can have the same knowledge and feeling about himself, because this involves nothing which depends on someone else" (Part III, art. 154; AT XI, 446; Cott. I, 384). The considerations that usually differentiate human beings—wealth, power, intelligence, knowledge, or beauty—all come to seem unimportant in contrast with the virtuous will. So, under the influence of *générosité*, we esteem ourselves without preferring ourselves to others.

Générosité represents a meeting point between the soul's passions, which originate in body, and thought. As a virtue, it is a habit in the soul which disposes it to have certain thoughts. The thoughts that virtuous habits produce in us may come from the soul alone. But they may be strengthened by the movement of the spirits, so that they are "both actions of virtue and at the same time passions of the soul" (Part III, art. 161; AT XI, 453; Cott. I, 387–88). Both understanding and will are involved in the retreat from the onslaught of the external into what is more truly the self. Volitions are the soul's principal activity. But they are grounded in judgments. The efficacy of the will is mediated through thought. Virtuous habits bring together our bodily and our mental being so that passions and thought meet. The passions are remedied through the operations of a will imbued with sound judgments of good and evil, the "proper arms" of the soul.

Descartes's view of the passions is thus more optimistic than it might at first appear from his talk of a retreat to what pertains to soul alone. The mind retreats in order to better engage with passion. And, although the passions can be destructive, they can also enable us to lead good and joyous lives, not merely as minds but as unions of mind and body. "The soul can have pleasures of its own. But the pleasures common to it and the body depend entirely on the passions, so that persons whom the passions can move most deeply are capable of enjoying the sweetest pleasures of this life. It is true that they may also experience the most bitterness when they do not know how to put these passions to good use and when fortune works against them. But the chief use of wisdom lies in teaching us to be masters of our passions and to control them with such skill that the evils which they cause are quite bearable, and even become a source of joy" (Part III, art. 212; AT XI, 488; Cott. I, 404). However, here as elsewhere, the uneasy union of mind and body is a weakness in Descartes's philosophy.[1] For Spinoza it is the flaw that renders the remedy for the passions unworkable.

Spinoza's 'Remedy': The Repudiation of the Will

In the preface to Part Five, Spinoza dismisses Descartes's idea that the will can redirect the course of the animal spirits by moving the pineal gland, as if it were like training a house dog to hunt or a hunting dog to refrain from chasing hares. The cumbersome story of a motivating force originating in the will and mediated through a firm judgment of good and evil, is replaced by a simpler one. In Part Three, Spinoza defines the passions as confused ideas, whereby the mind affirms of its body or of its parts a force of existing greater or less than before, and by the presence of which the mind is determined to think of one thing rather than another (IIIGen. Def. Aff.). This means that

---

1. For an interesting discussion of the issue of the coherence of Descartes's account of the passions, in relation to his treatment of the relations between mind and body, see Marjorie Grene, *Descartes* (Minneapolis: University of Minnesota Press, 1985), chapter 2, "Cartesian Passions: The Ultimate Incoherence," pp. 23–52.

Reason and the Passions

every passion has joy or sadness as an integral part. Joy is the transition to a greater state of activity or perfection, sadness the transition to a lesser (IIIDef. Aff. II and III).

Among the modifications of the body there are many that serve to increase or decrease its characteristic power of activity, its force for existing, while others neither enhance nor diminish it, bouncing off, as it were, without engaging with the body's endeavor to persist in being.[2] Since the mind is the idea of the body, the ideas of bodily transitions to greater or lesser states of activity are not a matter of indifference. "The idea of anything that increases or diminishes, aids or restrains, our Body's power of acting, increases or diminishes, aids or restrains, our Mind's power of thinking" (IIIP11). So there are transitions in the mind's power of acting—in its characteristic intensity. And these are Spinoza's versions of joy and sadness (IIIP11S). Out of them he reconstructs more specific emotions, each involving either joy or sadness, together with an associated idea of what is regarded as its cause.

Spinoza's version of the passivity involved in the passions centers on these ideas of causes. In the case of affects that are passions, the ideas are inadequate: here the mind is acted upon, so that its own activity is thwarted. The Cartesian distinction between intellectual joys or sorrows, on the one hand, and passions, on the other, undergoes a corresponding change. Where Descartes's distinction rests on the radical distinction between mind and body, Spinoza's is drawn in terms of the adequacy or inadequacy of the idea involved in the affect. And this yields a different picture of the role of reason. Reason

2. The importance of Spinoza's distinction between *affectus*—as "affect," implying transition in power of acting—and *affectio*—as mere bodily modification, implying the presence of an affecting body—is emphasized and elaborated by Gilles Deleuze in *Spinoza: Philosophie Pratique* (1981), pp. 68–69, translated by Robert Hurley as *Spinoza: Practical Philosophy* (San Francisco: City Lights Books, 1988), pp. 48–49. See also Edwin Curley's comment on the translation of *affectus,* in *The Collected Works of Spinoza* (Princeton: Princeton University Press, 1985), p. 625.

remedies the passions by replacing inadequate ideas of the body's transitions to greater or lesser states of activity by more adequate ones. The knowledge of good or evil, rather than mediating the virtuous will's transactions with body, now becomes supervenient on bodily change. It is nothing but "an affect of Joy or Sadness, insofar as we are conscious of it" (ivP8). The knowledge of good or evil follows necessarily from the affect of joy or sadness itself. It is no longer externally related to the affects but integrated into their very structure. The idea of an affect is united to the affect, he says, in the same way that mind is united to body. The idea is not really distinguished from the affect itself or from the idea of the body's affection, since, by the general definition of the affects, that is what the affect is (ivP8Dem).

All this means that there are conceptual connections between affects, the understanding of them, and the "knowledge of good and evil." The idea of the transition is only conceptually distinguished from the transition itself. And this provides the basis for Spinoza's version of the remedy of the passions through reason. Through understanding the affects, replacing the inadequate ideas they initially involve with more adequate ones, we do not simply retreat from the turmoil of passion into a realm of thought. The affect itself is transformed from a passion—an inadequate idea of a transition to a greater or lesser state of activity—to an active rational emotion, incorporating an adequate idea. So for Spinoza, in contrast to Descartes, the rational knowledge of good and evil is not an alternative source of motivation, competing with that of the affects. It is just our ideas of joy and sadness—different from the passions only in that it involves adequate ideas where they involve inadequate ones. The remedy for the passions resides in replacing the initially inadequate ideas of joy and sadness with adequate ones, thus passing from passivity to activity.

So it is precisely through understanding the passions that we become free of their oppressive force. Descartes failed to see that the very exercise of bringing the passions under the scope of rational understanding was the source of freedom. He superimposed on the understanding of the passions a cumbersome story of the will counteracting their force, under the influence of judgments of good and evil which come from elsewhere. Spinoza's version of reason engages directly with the passions through understanding them. For Descartes in the *Passions of the Soul* the "striving" that overcomes the passion was an act of will transcending the understanding—an effort to "correct our natural faults by striving to separate within ourselves the movements of the blood and spirits from the thoughts with which they are usually joined" (Part III, art. 211; AT XI, 486; Cott. 1, 403). For Spinoza it becomes not an act of will, imposed from above to disrupt our natural condition, but rather our natural state, now adequately understood. Our power to overcome the passions, far from being a mark of our transcendence of the necessities of nature, is the mark of our inclusion under them. Freedom from the bondage of passion comes from an understanding of the necessities that govern them. Before seeing exactly how this is supposed to happen, it will be helpful to look in more detail at how Spinoza's account of the "knowledge of good and evil" and its relations to the passions differs from that of Descartes.

The Classification of the Passions

Spinoza's classification of the passions simplifies that offered by Descartes. For both there are "primary affects" in terms of which the others are explained. But where Descartes had six primary affects—joy, sorrow, desire, wonder, love, and hate—Spinoza makes do with three—desire, joy, and sadness. Love and hate are explained in terms of joy and sadness, in association with the idea of an external cause. And wonder is not strictly an affect at all, since it does not involve any transition to greater or less activity. His three primary affects, moreover, have an interconnection that they lacked in the Cartesian scheme. Spinoza integrates them into his account of what it is to be an affect at all. "An Affect that is called a Passion of the mind is a confused idea, by which the Mind affirms of its Body, or of some part of it, a greater or lesser force for existing than before, which, when it is given, determines the Mind to think of this rather than that" (iiiGen. Def. Aff.).

In his explanation of the definition Spinoza comments that the affirmation of greater or less force of existing includes the nature of joy and sadness in the definition, while the reference to the determination of thought includes the nature of desire. Descartes had already stressed in the *Passions of the Soul* the close connections between desire and activity. But for him not all desire is an act of the soul. There are two forms of desire, related to activity in different ways. In opposition to the scholastics, he insisted that desire is, in one sense, a unitary emotion. Aversion is not a separate passion from desire. Desire has no opposite. It is always "one and the same movement," which gives rise to the pursuit of a good and at the same time the avoidance of the opposite evil, although the one kind of desire may be accompanied by different passions—love, hope, and joy in the one case; hatred, anxiety, and sadness in the other (Part ii, arts. 86, 87; AT xi, 392–93; Cott. i, 358–59).

Although Cartesian desire is in that way unitary, the sharpness of the distinction between mind and body demands that the concept of desire be, in another way, nonunitary. The desires that express the soul's own nature are themselves "acts" in a sense which he denies to the passion of desire, which depends on body. The soul's volitions are pure acts of the soul, unmediated through the movement of the animal spirits. The passion of desire, in contrast, is "an agitation of the soul caused by the spirits, which dispose the soul to wish, in the future, for the things it represents to itself as agreeable," whether it be the presence of goods that are absent, the preservation of those that are present, the absence of present or future evils (Part ii, art. 86; AT xi, 392–93; Cott. i, 358–59). It is this direction to the future which gives the passion of desire its centrality in Descartes's account of the motivation of embodied human action. The influence of other passions on our actions is mediated through the passion of desire. But the volitions of the soul are pure acts of the will, unmediated through body or passion.

In the lack of the Cartesian distinction between mind and body, Spinoza's version of desire becomes unitary in a stronger sense. Where Descartes distinguished desire as an act of the soul from desire as a passion, Spinoza speaks of one "striving," which may involve either adequate or inadequate ideas (IIIP9). The mind strives to persist in being and is conscious of this striving, both insofar as it has adequate ideas and insofar as it has inadequate ones. When this striving is related only to the mind, it is called will; when it is related to the mind and body together it is called appetite (IIIP9Dem). And desire is nothing more than this appetite, insofar as we are conscious of it. Will can still be thought of as pertaining to mind alone, whereas desire involves reference to body, but the underlying state is the same—a state of being determined to activity. So for Spinoza desire is neither a pure act of mind, able to causally influence body, nor a passive registering of a state produced by body. It is neither the Cartesian act of will nor the Cartesian passion, but a striving to act, which can be either active or passive, according as it involves adequate or inadequate ideas.

Joy and sadness, as we have seen, are integrated into Spinoza's version of the affects. And it is because this makes essential to an affect the transition to a greater or lesser state of activity that wonder is not strictly an affect. It involves, as Descartes observed, a kind of stasis in which we are surprised by novelty (Part II, art. 53; AT XI, 373; Cott. I, 350). Since this may happen before we know whether the object is beneficial or harmful, Descartes regards wonder as "the first of all the passions." It has no opposite, since "if the object before us has no characteristics that surprise us, we are not moved by it at all and we consider it without passion." It is this arrest of the soul's capacity for judgment that gives wonder its primary position in Descartes's classification of the emotions. It does not involve the consideration of good or evil, which differentiates the other passions. For Spinoza, in contrast, this stasis disqualifies wonder from being an affect. Because it is prior to any determination of the mind which could either impede or enhance its characteristic activity, it involves neither desire nor the dimension of joy or sadness, both of which are essential to Spinozistic affects.

Joy and sadness too stand in very different relations to desire and to the knowledge of good and evil from their Cartesian equivalents. For Descartes, joy, like desire, comes in two forms—one purely intellectual, the other produced in the soul by body. Intellectual joy is a pleasant emotion that the soul arouses in itself whenever it enjoys a good that its understanding represents to it as its own, and there is a corresponding intellectual sadness associated with perceived lack. But while the soul is united to body, this intellectual joy or sadness can scarcely fail to be accompanied by the other kind—the passion that ensues from the movement of the spirits. As soon as intellect perceives that we possess some good, even if it be one that has nothing to do with the body, the imagination forms an impression of it in the brain, from which ensues the movement of the spirits that produces the passion of joy (Part II, art. 91; AT XI, 397; Cott. I, 360). Joy and sadness, in both forms, involve the notions of good and evil; and are, in the well-functioning mind, subject to true knowledge of good and evil. For Spinoza, the "knowledge of good and evil" can have no such role of dominance.

Love, Hate, and the Knowledge of Good and Evil

Descartes's distinction between mind and body means that he must juggle distinctions between what is good or evil for the body, for the soul, and for their union, telling different causal stories for each case. These complex combinations of separateness and togetherness, resulting from the separation and uneasy union of mind and body, can be seen clearly in his treatment of love and hate. For him, unlike Spinoza, they are distinct "primary" passions. Love and hate are passions of the soul, caused by movements of the spirits, which impel the soul either to join itself with objects that appear agreeable or to separate itself from objects that appear harmful. The role of the spirits, he comments, distinguishes them from judgments, which also bring the soul to join itself with things or to separate itself from them, and from emotions produced directly in the soul by such judgments (Part II, art. 79; AT XI, 387; Cott. I, 356).

Passion and judgment, though separate, interact in love and hate. Our power of willingly joining or separating ourselves from something should not, Descartes stresses, be confused with the passion of desire. This power is rather to be understood as the soul's assent, by which the soul considers itself as forming a whole with what it finds agreeable. The soul takes itself to be only a part of that whole, and the thing loved to be the other part. In hate, the soul considers itself alone as a whole, entirely separated from the thing for which it has an aversion. Descartes's definitions of love and hate thus invoke the soul's assent, which pertains to it alone, as well as its causal interactions with body. Their "natural function" is to move the soul to consent and contribute to actions that promote the body's preservation and well-being (Part II, art. 137; AT XI, 430; Cott. I, 376). But our well-being as composites of mind and body can be at odds with our well-being as minds alone. Love and hate demonstrate both the union and the separateness of mind and body.

In the pursuit of our well-being as composites of mind and body, sadness takes priority over joy and hatred over love. It is more important to reject what can destroy us than to acquire those things that can enrich us; and an inappropriate love, joining us to things that may be harmful, is of more consequence than an inappropriate hatred. But the situation is reversed when we consider the function of the passions in relation to the soul. In this regard, love and hatred result from knowledge. And when that knowledge is true—when the things it brings us to love or hate are truly good or bad—love is better than hatred. It can never be too great and never fails to produce joy, for it joins us to real goods. All that the most excessive love could do is join us so perfectly to those goods that the love we have for ourselves applies to them as well. That must produce joy, for it represents to us what we love as a good belonging to us (Part II, art. 139; AT XI, 432; Cott. I, 377). With regard to what pertains to us as minds, self-love and love of the good come together, since we and it form a unity.

If we consider the soul apart from the body, Cartesian joy cannot fail to be good, nor sadness bad. If we had no body, we could not go too far in abandoning ourselves to love or joy, or in avoiding hatred and sadness. But the bodily movements accompanying these passions, although they are beneficial when moderate, may be injurious to health when they are very violent. Soul and body can pull in different directions. What is good for us as minds does not always coincide with what is good for us as composites. The uninterrupted pursuit of clear and distinct thought can damage us, as Descartes tells Elizabeth in his letter of 28 June 1643 (AT III, 690).[3] The mind-body union is an uneasy one. Although the body is only the lesser part of us, its presence must modify the wise pursuit of intellectual joys.

The passion of desire, if well controlled, can give us intimations of what a well-functioning union of mind and body might be like, with the body enhancing the soul's pleasures and the soul adapting its desires to take account of its union with body. When the soul was newly joined to the body, Descartes says wistfully (Part II, art. III; AT XI, 411; Cott. I, 367), all its first desires must have been to accept things beneficial to it, and to reject those harmful; and the spirits must have begun to move all the muscles and sense organs to those ends. That is why, when the soul now desires something, the whole body becomes more agile, and this in turn makes its desires stronger and keener. It is interesting to note in connection with Descartes's discussion of desire and love that his account elsewhere of the soul's relation with body coincides with his definition of love. He is, as he says in the Sixth

3. The letter is translated by Anthony Kenny in *Descartes: Philosophical Letters* (Oxford: Clarendon Press, 1970), pp. 140ff.

Meditation, so closely united with his body that he and it form a unity. But, despite his nostalgic glimpses of a lost harmony, it is, as we have seen, by and large a vexed and ambivalent love relationship.

For Spinoza the passions of joy and sadness cease to be differentiated from purely intellectual joys or sorrows by reference to the mind-body distinction, and this transforms their relation to the knowledge of good and evil. Rather than causally producing joy and sadness, the knowledge of good and evil now becomes supervenient on them. The knowledge of good and evil is nothing but the idea of joy or sadness that follows from the affect of joy or sadness. The relations between desire and the knowledge of good and evil are also reversed. For Descartes the knowledge of good and evil could produce the passion of desire. For Spinoza it is the other way round. From his account of will, appetite, and desire, it follows, he says, that "it is clear that we neither strive for, nor will, neither want, nor desire anything because we judge it to be good; on the contrary, we judge something to be good because we strive for it, will it, want it, and desire it" (iiiP9S).

Freedom and Self-Determination

We are now in a position to see just how different are these two pictures of the relations between reason and the passions. For Spinoza it is precisely through understanding the passions that we become free. But this is not a matter of leaving the affects behind. All the affects are related to joy, sadness, and desire; and desire is nothing but the striving to act. So "to every action to which we are determined from an affect which is a passion, we can be determined by reason, without that affect" (ivP59). The claim is not that we can be determined to act, without any affect. Nor is Spinoza saying that to act from reason is to act without affectivity. By "acting from reason" he means, he says, "nothing but doing those things which follow from the necessity of our nature, considered in itself alone" (ivP59Dem). To act from reason is to act without those affects that are passions; and for Spinoza it means to act without affects that incorporate inadequate ideas—affects that are inadequately understood. For Descartes the knowledge of good and evil is an extraneous source of motivation, competing with that of the affects. For Spinoza it is just the idea of joy or sadness—but it is an adequate idea, in contrast to the inadequate ones incorporated into the passions of joy or sadness.

The mind's essence consists in the endeavor to persist in thought. This striving, to the extent that we are conscious of it, is desire. But the determination to activity that it involves can have its causes either inside or outside our own nature. Our minds, both as inadequate ideas and as adequate ones, endeavor to persist in being, and we are conscious of this endeavor. But insofar as it involves inadequate ideas, we are acted on from outside. With our active thinking thwarted, we are forced into passivity. To the extent that our ideas are adequate, in contrast, we are active.

Spinoza's affects are thus determinations in which the mind, as idea of the body, is aware of transitions to greater or lesser states of activity. Insofar as that awareness involves inadequate ideas, the affects are passions. But the mind can make its ideas more adequate. The knowledge of good and evil can replace the inadequate idea of the transition to greater or less activity. We are then determined no longer through "an affect which is a passion," but through reason. Spinozistic reason is thus able to engage directly with the passions, transforming the inadequate ideas they involve into adequate ones. And the process is itself affective. Since it involves the mind's transition to a greater state of activity, it is by definition joyful.

Reason, in the sense in which it is equated with the knowledge of good and evil, thus involves understanding affects of joy and sadness. But even where its object is sadness, since it involves adequate rather than inadequate ideas of the transition to lesser activity, it is itself joyful. This is Spinoza's version of Descartes's point that intellectual joy—as in, for example, reading or watching a theatrical performance—can coincide with, and indeed originate in, emotions of sadness. But it is not removed from the passion of joy in the way that Descartes's intellectual joy was. The view of the mind as idea of body, rather than as a separate substance causally interacting with it, allows for a much more direct relationship between reason and the passions than was possible for Descartes. Reason's direct engagement with the passions, replacing adequate for inadequate ideas, means that reason is itself in the realm of emotion.

Descartes failed to see that his exercise of bringing the passions under the scope of rational understanding had in itself the potential for freedom. He needlessly superimposed on the understanding of the passions a cumbersome story of the will counteracting their force—a task for which the will must make use of judgments of good and evil which do not arise from the understanding of the passions themselves. For Descartes the striving that overcomes the passions was an act of will which transcends the understanding—an effort to correct the "faults" of nature. For Spinoza the striving is not an act of will imposed from above to disrupt our natural condition, but rather our natural state—now adequately understood. Our power to overcome the passions, far from being a mark of our transcendence of the necessities of nature, is the mark of our inclusion under them. Freedom from the bondage of passion comes out of an understanding of the necessities that govern them.

The key to Descartes's remedy for the passions was the mind's awareness of itself as not bound by the necessities that govern the rest of nature. The key to Spinoza's remedy lies in acknowledging that we are part of nature, that our passions follow the same laws as other things—an insight to which Descartes was drawn, but from the full consequences of which he withdrew under the influence of the idea of the mind as transcending nature. However, Spinoza avoids the consequences that Descartes feared—that the mind is bound by external causes and hence unfree. Self-determination remains. But it too is transformed into something very different from determination by a Cartesian will. Let us now see what it amounts to.

For Descartes to be self-determined is to belong in a completely different causal story from that of determination by external causes. For Spinoza the two states, although very different from one another, are interconnected. We become self-determined through understanding the causes that determine us. He does, it is true, say that to anything to which I am determined by an affect that is a passion, I can also be determined by reason without that passion. But this does not mean that reason is a separate motivating force from passion, like the Cartesian will. Spinoza's point is rather that, for any determinate state in which the mind is affected by passion, reason can transform that passion by replacing the inadequate idea it involves with a more adequate one. Elaborating this point, Spinoza stresses that all the appetites or desires are passions only insofar as they arise from inadequate ideas and are counted as virtues when they are aroused or generated by adequate ideas. "For all the Desires by which we are determined to do something can arise as much from adequate ideas as from inadequate ones" (vp4S). It is the contrast between inadequacy and adequacy that is crucial. The mind's power of thinking and forming adequate ideas is its remedy for the affects.

When Spinoza talks of our being determined to do something first from passion and then from reason, his point is not that we can go out and perform from reason the same action to which we might be impelled by passion. It is not as if the mob that, under the influence of passion, massacred the de Witt brothers might instead have performed the same action from reason. The point is rather that, finding ourselves in a state of joy or sadness, we can replace the inadequate ideas involved with adequate ones, so that a passion is transformed into an active, rational emotion. So passions of joy are transformed into more durable joys, which are still affects, though no longer passions. As for a passion of sadness, he says, insofar as we understand its causes it ceases to be a passion and, to that extent, ceases to be sadness (vp18S).

Through understanding its passions the mind moves from passivity into activity and freedom. "Each of us has—in part, at least, if not absolutely—the power to understand himself and his affects, and consequently, the power to bring it about that he is less acted on by them" (vP4S). But reason is in this way effective against the passions only because it is itself affective. "No affect can be restrained by the true knowledge of good and evil insofar as it is true, but only insofar as it is considered as an affect" (ivP14). The activity of a mind in a state of passion is thwarted, for it has only inadequate ideas of its transitions to greater or lesser activity. In this respect the mind is acted upon rather than acting, even where it is in a state of joy. But this thwarted activity can be set free. The mind can disengage from the passivity and become active through understanding without losing contact with the original transition to a greater or lesser state of activity, which remains the object of its understanding. This is Spinoza's version of Descartes's theme of the disengagement from the passions. But unlike Descartes's version, the disengagement retains the structure of the original emotion, while replacing its idea component with a more adequate idea.

The capacity to understand the passions thus provides a spectrum for variation in the mind's activity. Spinoza, as we have seen, defines affects as complexes of bodily modifications, involving transitions to greater or lesser states of activity, together with the ideas of those transitions. As idea of the body, the mind's *conatus*, its essence, consists in being an active articulation and affirmation of body, and hence of itself. To the extent that it achieves this understanding, its own activity and perfection are enhanced. To the extent that it is thwarted in its endeavor to understand, its own activity and perfection are diminished. The mind thus has its own joys and sadness, associated with transition to greater or lesser self-understanding, and reflection on those transitions. "When the Mind considers itself and its power of acting, it rejoices, and does so the more distinctly it imagines itself and its power of acting" (iiiP53). The mind's essence affirms only what the mind is and can do. It is of its nature to imagine only those things that posit its own power of acting. This yields Spinoza's version of Descartes's distinction between "interior" and "exterior" emotions.

In its endeavor to maintain its own power of acting, the mind does not simply reflect the body's vicissitudes. It has its own struggle, grounded in those of the body, but with its own dynamism. And since the mind's power of acting resides in the striving to understand, even its own passivities can provide occasions for intellectual joy. For Spinoza however these intellectual joys cannot be separated off into a different realm to which mind might retreat. As ideas they remain connected with bodily transitions, which are their primary object, even though as joys they diverge from those original ideas. Thus an intellectual joy can have as its object a bodily transition to a lesser state of activity. Mind's efforts to more adequately understand ideas of transition to lesser states of activity can be a transition to greater activity and hence a joy. But, when this happens, the intellectual joy is not externally related to the passion but integrated with it.

To the extent that the mind's endeavor to understand is thwarted, it will undergo sadness, even in the midst of the passion of joy. So we have here a new field of variations, interlocking with that of the passions but not simply mirroring it. An active affect can be an understanding of a transition to lesser activity; and a passion can be a state of awareness, not clearly understood, of transition to greater activity. These dynamic variations in the mind's power of acting allow Spinoza to treat reason as having power to transform human life precisely through its affectivity. The mind cannot have true ideas without knowing that it has them. And its awareness of true ideas increases its activity. To the extent that the mind feels those transitions unimpeded, it rejoices. To the extent that it feels them thwarted, it is saddened.

There are echoes of Descartes's intellectual joys and sorrows in Spinoza's talk of the affects of joy and desire, distinguished from the passions of the same name by the fact that they are "related to us insofar as we act" (IIIP58). His remedy for the passions, like Descartes's, involves strengthening those affects that are more closely identified with ourselves, accentuating the connections between thought and desire. But there is a different basis for these connections. The mind's striving to persist in being is, by definition, desire. Therefore desire is related to us insofar as we understand or insofar as we act (IIIP58Dem). There is no struggle of will needed to bring desire and thought together. Thought has become conative and affective. And it is this, rather than the mere presence of truth, that allows reason to have power over the passions. It is only through being itself affective that reason can engage with the passions.

Descartes's strategy for dealing with harmful passions involved developing reason as an alternative, competing with the passions for our interest and allegiance. Spinoza's strategy is, in contrast, a matter of understanding and utilizing the affective nature of reason, which is implicit in every passion through the mind's capacity to transform inadequate ideas into adequate ones. Every state of passion can be transformed through understanding into an active rational affect that will increase our power of joyous activity, rendering us active rather than passive. We come to act from reason, not through acknowledging the shortcomings of emotion as a source of action, but rather through our determinate states being understood through our own nature.

The striking—and, for us Cartesians, counterintuitive—thing here is that determination by external causes does not rule out self-determination. For Spinoza these are two ways of understanding the same truth. "All our strivings, or Desires, follow from the necessity of our nature in such a way that they can be understood either through it alone, as through their proximate cause, or insofar as we are a part of nature, which cannot be conceived adequately through itself without other individuals" (IVApp, sec. 1). Freedom resides in moving from the latter state to the former. But this shift from passivity to activity does not alter the truth of the dependence of our strivings on external causes, or our vulnerability to them. Human beings are both part of nature and free—the two claims that Descartes saw as incompatible. Descartes thought that we should cultivate a lack of concern for "external" circumstances. Lying beyond the control of our wills, they are irrelevant to our moral well-being. There are echoes of this in Spinoza. But, here again, the point is subtly transformed. What comes about through our own nature must be good. That is to say, nothing evil can happen to us except through external causes." Because all those things of which man is the efficient cause must be good, nothing evil can happen to a man except by external causes, viz. insofar as he is a part of the whole of nature, whose laws human nature is compelled to obey, and to which it is forced to accommodate itself in ways nearly infinite" (IV App, sec. 6).

Spinoza agrees with Descartes that evil comes to us only insofar as we are subjected to external causes—only insofar as we are part of nature. But he believes that we are wholly part of nature and that this is consistent with understanding what happens to us as happening through our own nature. There is for him no incompatibility between necessity and freedom. Our capacity to attain freedom, however, is limited. Although any one passion can be transformed into rational emotion, there is no possibility of absolute freedom from the passions. "It is impossible that a man should not be a part of Nature, and that he should be able to undergo no changes except those which can be understood through his own nature alone, and of which he is the adequate cause" (IVP4). The point is that, although each determination can be truly apprehended in either way, it is not possible to grasp all our determinations actively and thus as determined through our own nature. For human power is limited. Every determination can be construed in either way. We can shift from the one way to the other for any one of them, but not for all.

For Spinoza then there is no specifiable set of determinations of which we can be the adequate cause, while others remain beyond the reach of freedom. Each of our determinations can be truly apprehended in either way. To understand what happens to us as determined through our own nature is not to offer a competing explanation from its determination by external causes, but to grasp the same truth in a more reflective way. The causes of the modifications remain external, but in understanding them we increase our own power and self-knowledge. It remains true that the original passivity was externally caused, but the passivity itself has now given way to activity. However no mind can accomplish that liberating transition for all its passions.

Descartes regarded us as autonomous rational wills, able in principle to choose our destiny, but contingently mixed in with bodies—uneasy, vulnerable interminglings, but capable of clearly apprehending the difference between our status as minds, and as unions with body, and of conducting our lives accordingly. He urged us to exert the power of our wills to overcome the "natural faults" that afflict us as interminglings. For Spinoza, in contrast, the truth of our existence is to be part of nature, from which it follows that we are necessarily always subject to passions, that we follow and obey the common order of nature, and accommodate ourselves to it as much as the nature of things requires (ivP4C). The fact that we are frequently overcome by passion, like the related fact that human power is ultimately outweighed at death by external causes, is not due to a fault in our own nature. It is just a consequence of our being fully part of nature.

Because human power is limited, "infinitely surpassed by the power of external causes," we do not have "absolute power to adapt things outside us to our use" (ivApp, sec. 32). There is no absolute freedom, for the same reasons that make it impossible for the mind to have only ideas that are adequate. It is always possible to make our ideas more adequate. But our status as part of nature makes it impossible that all our ideas should be totally adequate at all times. There is nonetheless much to be hoped for from the recognition of the truth that we are indeed part of nature. This truth comes, ironically, to occupy for Spinoza the central role in rightful self-esteem that for Descartes was occupied by free will. Reason remains the basis for self-esteem; the better part of us is the one given over to the understanding. But whereas for Descartes the "lesser" part is body, for Spinoza it is the portion of the mind which comprises inadequate ideas. What makes some minds more virtuous than others is the comparative strength of their capacity to understand their passions. "The power of the Mind is defined by knowledge alone, whereas lack of power, or passion, is judged solely by the privation of knowledge, i.e., by that through which ideas are called inadequate" (vP20S). So the virtue and power of a mind is defined by the power of its knowledge of its passions. We are in the grip of passion to the extent that adequate ideas of joy and sadness predominate over inadequate ones. That mind is "most acted on" of which inadequate ideas constitute the greatest part, so that "it is distinguished more by what it undergoes than by what it does." An active mind may have as many inadequate ideas as does a passive one, but they do not form the greater part of it.

Self-knowledge remains central for Spinoza. The first foundation of virtue is preserving one's being and doing this from the guidance of reason. "Therefore, he who is ignorant of himself is ignorant of the foundation of all the virtues, and consequently, of all the virtues" (ivP56Dem). Self-esteem remains the highest thing for which we can hope. And reason retains its central place in self-esteem. But the reason on which we rightly esteem ourselves is no longer grounded in a rational will, but in the power of understanding alone. Spinoza defines self-esteem (ivP52Dem) as "a Joy born of the fact that man considers himself and his power of acting" (ivP52Dem). But the true power of acting, he adds, is reason itself. So self-esteem arises from reason. While a man considers himself, he perceives nothing clearly and distinctly, or adequately, except "those things which follow from his power of acting," that is, from his power of understanding. So the greatest possible self-esteem arises from this reflection. He adds in the Scholium that self-esteem is really the highest thing we can hope for. For no one strives to preserve his being for the sake of any end. But whereas for Descartes the connections between self-esteem and reason mean that self-esteem centers on knowing our separateness from the rest of nature, for Spinoza it centers on knowing that is not the case.

Something remains of the Cartesian ideal of autonomous selfhood. The human being who is led by passion, whether he wills it or not, does "those things he is most ignorant of," whereas the one who is free from passion complies with no one's wishes but his own, doing only those things he knows to be most important in life and desires very greatly. "Hence, I will call the former a slave, but the latter, a free man" (ivP66S). The character ideal that Spinoza presents as arising from this self-understanding has some strong echoes too of Cartesian *générosité:* "a man strong in character hates no one, is angry with no one, envies no one, is indignant with no one, scorns no one, and is not at all proud." But this detachment is, again, grounded in the antithesis of Descartes's autonomous will. "A man strong in character considers this most of all, that all things follow from the necessity of the divine nature" (ivP73S).

There are echoes of Descartes in Spinoza's description of the right attitude toward doing our duty. We shall, he says, "bear calmly those things which happen to us contrary to what the principle of our advantage demands, if we are conscious that we have done our duty, that the power we have could not have extended itself to the point where we could have avoided those things, and that we are a part of the whole of nature, whose order we follow" (iv App, sec. 32). But his version of detachment lacks the dourness of the Cartesian version. For him rightful self-esteem is grounded in the singularity of selves, in their reflection on their striving to persist in being—which distinguishes them from one another—rather than on what they have in common. For Descartes, as later for Kant, self-esteem is founded on what minds have in common, on that wherein humans transcend the rest of nature. For Spinoza it is founded rather on the particularities of existence, on the affects that move us individually to joy and sadness. "Though each individual lives content with his own nature, by which he is constituted, and is glad of it, nevertheless that life with which each one is content, and that gladness, are nothing but the idea, or soul, of the individual. And so the gladness of the one differs in nature from the gladness of the other as much as the essence of the one differs from the essence of the other" (IIIP57S). This may seem at odds with Spinoza's concern, later in the text, with shared human nature as the proper object of moral concern. Insofar as men live according to the guidance of reason, he says at IVP35Dem, they must do only those things that are good for human nature, and hence, for each man. But even here it is clear that Spinoza is not privileging human nature over individual human beings. Individuals who share our nature are important to us—but not because they enable us to transcend either our own or their individuality. We transcend self-interest in the concern for others who share our nature. But we are concerned for those individuals, not just for the nature we share with them. In doing what is "good for human nature," we do those things that agree with the nature of each man. Individual well-being is not replaced but enhanced by what is in harmony with our shared nature (IVP31C). And in this delight in our shared nature there is no escape from the necessity that governs the rest of the world.

Descartes's version of tranquillity of spirit had as its rationale that some things are under the mind's control, others not, and that we can know the difference between the two. Spinoza, I think with conscious irony, has transformed the thought of "the celebrated Descartes," so that the fully free human beings are those who know that they can control nothing, but feel none the worse for that.

FOUR

O

Intuitive Knowledge and the
Eternity of the Mind

Spinozistic freedom comes from the understanding of the passions.
But what kind of understanding is this? For a contemporary
reader one of the most puzzling things about the *Ethics* is the apparent
ease with which Spinoza moves between theoretical understanding of
the passions—on the model of lines and bodies, as he describes it in
the preface to Part Three—and a more direct, personal reflection on
passion in the midst of the turmoil it induces in us. There is no
distinction here of the kind Descartes draws between practical knowledge—the knowledge of pleasure and pain that concerns us as "interminglings"—and the understanding of the natures of things that
comes from clear and distinct thinking. For Spinoza, reflection on
bodily modifications in their immediacy does not lead down a path of
practical knowledge, carefully marked off from the high road of
theoretical understanding. It leads directly into the highest forms of
knowledge—subsumed into them, but never left behind. This is a pattern of relationship between the lower and higher forms of knowledge
which, we shall see, has some affinities with Hegel's description of the
development of self-consciousness in the *Phenomenology of Spirit,* in
contrast with our own familiar distinctions between impersonal scientific knowledge and reflection on life, which are more Cartesian in
spirit. Reflection on the passions and their contribution to life finds
expression more in contemporary literature than in philosophy.

Part of Nature

We have seen that the capacity of the human body to retain traces of modification makes possible both error and the formation of the common notions of reason. It also makes possible the highest kind of knowledge—intuition, the intellectual love of God which yields the eternity of the mind. Whereas for Descartes immortality rested on the separability of mind from body, for Spinoza the mind's eternity is founded in its status as idea of a body with a wide variety of capacities. "He who has a Body capable of a great many things has a Mind whose greatest part is eternal" (vP39). Bodily complexity, self-knowledge and the eternity of the mind belong together. "Because human Bodies are capable of a great many things, there is no doubt but that they can be of such a nature that they are related to Minds which have a great knowledge of themselves and of God, and of which the greatest, or chief, part is eternal. So they hardly fear death" (vP39S).

Spinoza, we have also seen, takes much further than Descartes the idea of the affectivity of reason. Reason involves the mind's transitions to a greater state of activity and hence joy. These joys, though intellectual, are grounded in the powers and pleasures of bodies. And the common notions of reason are grounded in imagination and conceived in joy. They arise, as Deleuze has pointed out, from primitive states of joy in which the mind grasps relations of congeniality between its own and other bodies.[1] Our understanding of what bodies have in common arises from experience of their affinities—a joy that precedes our efforts to understand it. So there are continuities between imagination, in which the mind is aware of present and past bodily modifications; joy, in which the mind is aware of transitions to greater states of activity; and reason, in which the mind forms common notions of the

1. For an interesting discussion of this affective dimension of Spinoza's treatment of the common notions, see Gilles Deleuze, "Spinoza et nous," *Actes du Colloque International Spinoza,* Paris, 3–5 May 1977 (Paris: Albrui Michel, 1978); published also as chapter 6 of his *Spinoza: Philosophie pratique* (Paris: Minuit, 1981), pp. 164–75; translated by Robert Hurley as *Spinoza: Practical Philosophy* (San Francisco: City Lights Books, 1988), pp. 122–30.

affinities of bodies. These continuities flow on into Spinoza's highest kind of knowledge. What is it, and how does it differ from reason?

Intuitive Knowledge

The idea of a direct, unmediated form of knowledge—a kind of mental vision—has a long philosophical history.[2] It is present in Descartes's theory of knowledge, although it is only in his early work, the *Rules for the Direction of the Mind,* that he calls it "intuition." There are some similarities between his concept of intuition there and Spinoza's intuitive knowledge, although it is not certain that Spinoza would have had access to the *Rules.* In Rule Three Descartes presents intuition as, like deduction, an "action of the intellect," by means of which we are able to arrive at a knowledge of things without fear of being mistaken. In contrast to the "fluctuating testimony of the senses" and the "deceptive judgment of the imagination as it botches things together," intuition is the "conception of a clear and attentive mind" which proceeds solely from the light of reason (AT x, 368; Cott. 1, 14). He contrasts it with deduction, as a more basic intellectual act that lacks the "movement or a sort of sequence" involved in deduction. But it is no less a product of reason. Descartes's "intuition" is not contrasted with reason but defined in terms of it. The distinction is a temporal one. Deduction relies on memory and thus lacks the immediate self-evidence of intuition. But if deduction is performed through a "continuous and uninterrupted movement of thought in which each individual proposition is clearly intuited," it can have the same immunity to error (AT x, 370; Cott. 1, 15). And deduction can come to approximate to intuition, as he shows in Rule Eleven. It is only when we think of it as a movement of thought rather than as a completed

2. See Harry A. Wolfson, *The Philosophy of Spinoza* (1934; New York: Meridian, 1958), vol. 2, chap. 16, pp. 155ff. for an informative discussion of pre-Cartesian versions of this idea.

process, that deduction can really be distinguished from intuition. If we think of deduction as a completed movement, rater than as the movement itself, the distinction disappears (AT x, 408; Cott. 1, 37).

Metaphors of light and vision pervade Descartes's treatment of intuition. He makes the comparison explicit at Rule Nine. We can best learn, he says there, how mental intuition is to be employed by comparing it with ordinary vision. If one tries to look at many objects at one glance, one sees none of them distinctly. Likewise, if we attend to too many things at the same time in a single act of thought, we do so with confused minds. Craftsmen who engage in delicate operations, fixing their eyes on a single point, acquire the ability to make perfect distinctions between even minute and delicate things. The same is true of those thinkers who devote their attention to the simplest and easiest of matters, never letting their thinking be distracted by many different objects at the same time. It is in keeping with the comparison with sight that Descartes claims that intuition is much more common than might be thought. All of us can mentally intuit that we exist, that we are thinking, that a triangle is bounded by three sides, and so on. Because we think of intuition as something complex and difficult, we underestimate the extent of our knowledge, giving too much credence to the "sublime and far-fetched arguments of the philosophers," as if there were "more clarity in darkness than in light" (AT x, 401; Cott. 1, 33).

Spinoza's intuitive knowledge has continuities with Descartes's notion of direct apprehension by an attentive mind. But it is for Spinoza distinct from the knowledge gained through reason. Whereas reason has no access to individuals, intuition has special associations with the knowledge of individuals and, especially, with self-knowledge. It is associated also with the knowledge of the attributes of God, and its connections with love go beyond the general ones between reason and affectivity.

Some aspects of the distinction between reason and intuition had already been formulated in the *Short Treatise*. There Spinoza talks of a form of clear knowledge, involving an immediate enjoyment of objects—a form of understanding that has in this respect more affinity with imagination and passions than reason. Spinoza elaborates the distinction through the same example of the rule of three that he uses in the *Ethics*. Knowledge through calculation goes beyond knowledge based on following a rule, which he compares to the knowledge a blind man has of color, repeating information "as a parrot repeats what it has been taught." Knowledge based on calculation is in turn surpassed by reason, which grasps the implications of the property of proportionality. But the clearest form of knowledge goes beyond report, experience, and even the "art of reasoning"—a "penetration" through which the proportionality in all the calculations is immediately seen (Part II, chap. 1; G. 1/54; C. 96–98).

The *Ethics* version of the example does not correspond exactly to that in the *Short Treatise*. Merchants, he says, find the fourth proportional by following a rule they have been taught, or by unreflective extrapolation from something they know from the simplest numbers. In this knowledge of the first kind, we rely on opinion, trusting to the authority of others; or merely on imagination, projecting without understanding from past experience. But merchants might instead find the required number through the force of demonstration of the relevant proposition in Euclid, that is, from the common property of proportions. They would in this case be knowing through common notions, through an understanding of what different cases have in common. This illustrates knowledge of the second kind, reason. Finally, there are the cases where we simply "see," as in the case of the simplest numbers. Knowledge of this third kind, Spinoza says, disconcertingly, proceeds from "an adequate idea of the formal essence of certain attributes of God to the adequate knowledge of the essence of things" (IIP40S2).

When Spinoza comes back to the topic in Part Five, the immediacy of intuition takes on special connections with the specificity of things, which eludes reason's grasp of general truths through common notions. Intuitive knowledge does not always have individuals as its object. It is, after all, introduced with reference to mathematical truths. But even where its objects are not individual, intuition is directed to the specificity of a case, rather than simply grasping a case as falling under or contained in a general rule. Unlike reason, it can reach the individual, rather than stopping short at the common notion. And, where it does, intuition's engagement with the actuality of things is more powerful than can be gained through reason. Hence its special power and affective force. It is this capacity to engage directly with existence that makes intuition both the highest kind of knowledge and the highest form of affectivity—the "intellectual love of God." Knowledge gained through reason is adequate knowledge. Since the common notions that are its proper objects are "equally in the whole and in the part," reason is not subject to the fragmentation that makes the lowest kind of knowledge open to error. Yet reason is an imperfect form of knowledge in comparison with intuition. For reason fails to capture of itself how the essences known through common notions are related to existence. The superiority of intuitive knowledge over reason resides, it seems, largely in the fact that it better reflects the distinctive connections between Spinozistic essence and existence.

Essence and Existence

For Spinoza the essences of finite things are separate from their existence. This is the mark of their difference from substance. But there is nonetheless a way in which they are not detachable from existence. This nondetachability of essence from existence represents a crucial departure from earlier treatments of essence. Like Descartes, Spinoza sees the true unity of essence and existence as applying only to God, and it is the lack of this unity in finite things that makes them dependent on God. But the difference between finite things and God in relation to the essence-existence distinction amounts to something very different for Spinoza, reflecting his transformation of the notion of substance. Spinoza stresses that essence is not merely that without which the thing would not be—that which "being taken away, the thing is necessarily taken away"—but also that which "being given, the thing is necessarily given." Spinoza's essence is not just "that without which the thing can neither be nor be conceived," but also "that which can neither be nor be conceived without the thing" (11Def2).

There is then for Spinoza a kind of inseparability of essence and existence which applies to finite things. But it is an inseparability of a very different kind from that involved in substance. This form of inseparability of essence and existence is in fact required in order to preserve the distinctive status of substance. It is his doctrine that finite things are modes of substance that necessitates the extra condition on the notion of essence—that where essence is given, the thing is given. Since he thinks human beings can neither be nor be conceived without substance, the more standard definition of essence, he explains, would demand that substance be of their essence. They would then, like substance, be necessarily existent (11P10Dem). The problem did not arise for the older accounts. On the more traditional definition, essence was just that without which a thing could neither be nor be conceived. But this was accompanied by a view of finite things as able to be conceived, though not to actually exist, without God. So the restricted definition of essence did not have the consequence that the existence of finite things became necessary. The additional condition allows Spinoza to distinguish between the necessary existence of substance and the modal status of finite things (11P10S). With this distinction assured, he is then able to say that the existence of finite things is nonetheless necessary, though in a different way from that of substance. Their existence follows from the nature of substance, just as truths about the triangle follow from its nature (1P17S1). Their existence is necessary in that it follows from the necessary existence of substance. But this does not mean that substance is of their essence. They are not substance, though they do necessarily follow from substance.

So Spinoza defines essence as unable to be or to be conceived without the thing, as well as being that without which the thing can neither be nor be conceived. An essence cannot be given without the thing itself being given. Spinozistic "essence," as he defines it in Part Two, is more specific than the shared "natures" he sometimes speaks of as given by the definitions of things, as in 1P7S2, or as the object of moral concern in the passage already discussed (1vP35Dem). At 1P17S2 he follows the usage he goes on to reject in his own definition of essence in Part Two, saying that two men "can agree entirely according to their essence" so that the perishing of one of them does not destroy the shared essence. In Part Two, where he is more concerned with issues of individuality, essences are firmly anchored in existence— neither beings of thought nor the general intelligible natures of things abstracted from existence, in the manner of the scholastic forms.

This theme of the inseparability of essence and existence in finite things was already present in the "Appendix Containing Metaphysical Thoughts" to Spinoza's *Descartes's "Principles of Philosophy."* There essence and existence are treated as contrasting ways of construing created things, and both of them are distinct from the mere "being of ideas." The "being of essence" is "nothing but that manner in which created things are comprehended in the attributes of God." And the "being of existence" is "the essence itself of things outside God, considered in itself." It is "attributed to things after they have been created by God" (Part 1, chap. 2; G. 1/238; C. 304). Even here we can see the special connections between essence, actual existence, and God, although they are elaborated differently in the *Ethics.* If the things we seek to understand had not been already created, he says, it would be impossible to understand their essences without an adequate knowledge of the nature of God—just as impossible as knowing the nature of the coordinates of a parabola prior to a knowledge of its nature (Part 1, chap. 2; G. 1/239; C. 305).

In the *Metaphysical Thoughts* Spinoza seems rather blandly confident of the clarity of the notion of essence, claiming that it can readily be grasped from the mere fact that we are familiar with giving definitions. To bother with other authors' definitions or descriptions of essence and existence would "render a clear thing more obscure." "Since we can give no definition of anything without at the same time explaining its essence, what do we understand more clearly than what essence is, and what existence is?" (Part I, chap. 2; G. I/239; C. 305). But his stress on the inseparability of the essences of finite things from actual existence is a departure from the familiar notion of essence manifested in the giving of definitions. Descartes had already moved in this direction with his repudiation of the scholastic substantial forms as proper objects of knowledge: there are no intelligible general natures abstractable from existence in extension that might pass over into the mind. But his rejection of the separability of essence from its existence in extension falls short of Spinoza's. That essence can be given without the thing itself being given, can indeed be seen as central to the method of doubt. Cartesian essences are not mere beings of thought. And our ideas of essences are not subjective or arbitrary. When I imagine a triangle, even if perhaps "no such figure exists, or has ever existed, anywhere outside my thought," there is still a "determinate nature" that is "immutable and eternal, and not invented by me or dependent on my mind (Fifth Meditation, AT VII, 64; Cott. II, 44–45)." There need be nothing outside the mind in which those determinate natures are embodied. Descartes needs the veracious God to ensure that they reside in something actually existing.

Gassendi challenged this way of thinking of essence, suggesting that the being of essence was really just a being of thought. "You will say," he says, "that all that you are proposing is the scholastic point that the natures or essences of things are eternal, and that eternally true propositions can be asserted of them. But this is just as hard to accept; and in any case it is impossible to grasp how there can be a human nature if no human being exists." "The schoolmen," he continues, "say that talking of the essence of things is one thing and talking of their existence is another, and that although things do not exist from eternity their essences are eternal. But in that case, since the most important element in things is their essence, does God do anything very impressive when he produces their existence? Is he doing anything more than a tailor does when he tries a suit of clothes on someone?" (Objections 5, AT VII, 319; Cott. II, 222).

Hobbes also refused to see the Cartesian idea of essence without existence as anything more than a "mental fiction" (Objections 3, AT VII, 194; Cott. II, 136). Spinoza keeps the distinction between essence and existence, but in a way that accords with the spirit of Hobbes's repudiation of abstract essences. His insistence that, where essence is, there must existence be, comes much closer to Hobbes than Descartes could have allowed without abandoning his method of doubt. Spinozistic eternal essences could not be said to become actual in the manner of a tailor putting a suit of clothes on a customer. The understanding of essences becomes a way of understanding things as actually existing. The result, as we shall see, is a distinctive conception of how we apprehend essences as eternal.

Eternity and Duration

To understand the essence of a thing as eternal is for Spinoza a way of understanding the thing as actual. He presents this special way of understanding actual existence as the climax of the *Ethics*. It is the highest kind of knowledge and the mind's highest form of freedom, virtue, and blessedness. Through intuitive knowledge we come to understand the actual existence of things with reference to the idea of God. What does this involve? Spinoza distinguishes it from the more mundane way of understanding a thing as actual at vP29S. We think of a thing as actual, he says there, in two ways: either we conceive it to exist "in relation to a certain time and place," or we conceive it to be "contained in God and to follow from the necessity of the divine nature." Things we conceive in this second way as true or real, he adds, we conceive "under a species of eternity," and to that extent they involve the "eternal and infinite essence of God." The first way involves perceiving things as durational, the second perceives them as eternal. But each is a true perception. And, far from being in conflict, the two are interconnected. The second way of perceiving the thing as actual provides a basis for understanding what is involved in its duration—its existence in time.

When we understand a finite thing "under a species of eternity," we understand its essence. But, given Spinoza's treatment of the relations between essence and existence, this involves understanding that it must exist in time. We understand a finite thing as depending on substance for its continued existence; for that is what is involved in its being a mode. When we understand it as actual in the first way, in contrast, what we understand is a consequence of its being the kind of thing that depends on substance. We understand its existence in relation to other such conditioned beings—its place in the network of finite modes in space and time. The contrast is between understanding the thing's metaphysical character—its dependence on substance— and, on the other hand, understanding its present actual existence— determining, and determined by, other finite modes.

Spinoza's treatment of the relations between duration and dependence echoes a theme from Descartes's Third Meditation, where he points out that created things depend on God just as much for their continued existence as for their beginning to be. From the fact that he existed a little while ago, it does not follow, Descartes says, that he exists now, unless there is some cause which, as it were, creates him afresh at this moment (AT vii, 48; Cott. ii, 33). In answering the first set of objections, Descartes elaborates on the connections between this idea of constant creation and the view of time as breaking up into separable divisions (AT vii, 109; Cott. ii, 78–79). He makes a similar point in the systematized version of the argument for the existence of God, at the end of the second set of replies, presenting it as an axiom that "there is no relation of dependence between the present time and the immediately preceding time, and hence no less a cause is required to preserve something than is required to create it in the first place"

(AT vii, 165; Cott. ii, 116). It is this idea of a prolongation of existence that Spinoza builds into his treatment of finite modes.

The Cartesian echoes are strong in the discussion of duration in the *Metaphysical Thoughts*. There Spinoza links duration with the separability of essence from existence in created things. Duration cannot pertain to the essences of things as such. But the dependence of created things on God involves a separation of essence from existence. This makes it appropriate to say that created things "enjoy" existence—a phrase that is strictly inapplicable to God, in whom there is no separation of essence and existence. Echoing Descartes, Spinoza adds that all created things, while they enjoy present duration and existence, altogether lack future duration and existence, "because it must continually be attributed to them" (Part ii, chap. i; G. 1/252; C. 318). In God, in contrast, there is no possibility of the kind of "existence in stages" appropriate to conditioned things. Spinoza connects this idea of dependence on a force not our own for our prolongation in existence with the idea of "having life," a locution that depends on the fact that the force through which things persevere is distinct from the things themselves (Part ii, chap. 6; G. 1/260; C. 326).

Against this background it becomes clear how in the *Ethics* Spinoza can present his two ways of understanding a thing as actual as not being at odds with one another. To understand the thing in relation to the idea of God is to understand the basis of its continued existence. And although the two kinds of understanding are interconnected, neither can be reduced to the other. Eternity cannot be understood in terms of duration. It is "existence itself, insofar as it is conceived to follow necessarily from the definition alone of the eternal thing" (1Def8). Only substance is thus eternal. But finite things can be understood with reference to eternity. "Eternity is the very essence of God insofar as this involves necessary existence. . . . To conceive things under a species of eternity, therefore, is to conceive things insofar as they are conceived through God's essence, as real beings, or insofar as through God's essence they involve existence" (vP30Dem). Duration, similarly, is defined in terms of the existence appropriate to modes. It is an "indefinite continuation of existing" (11Def5).

In the *Metaphysical Thoughts*, duration is only "distinguished by reason" from the existence of created things. "For as you take duration away from the thing, you take away just as much of its existence" (Part 1, chap. 4; G. 1/244; C. 310). The *Ethics* version of eternity and duration echoes the version in the *Metaphysical Thoughts* and the Cartesian themes that inspired it. In both works the distinction between eternity and duration is superimposed on that between the existence of substance and the existence of modes. Given the radical character of that distinction, it may seem strange that finite modes can be understood as actual, both in terms of duration and in terms of eternity. But in fact there is no conflict here. What it is to be eternal cannot be understood in terms of duration. In understanding a thing as eternal we do not understand it as lasting forever. And insofar as we understand a thing in relation to the spatio-temporal network in which it is located, we do not understand it as eternal.

The *Metaphysical Thoughts* is of course no guide to Spinoza's mature thought. But the theme of the radical distinction between eternity and duration recurs in the *Ethics*, reflecting again the different kinds of existence of substance and finite things. Here too the distinction turns not on the extent of time over which a unitary kind of existence holds, but on the kind of existence. Eternity and duration are defined in terms of the existence of substance and modes respectively. But now, in understanding the dependence on substance which makes the finite thing durational, we understand that mode as itself eternal. This would of course contradict the whole idea of the two kinds of existence, if it meant that we thought of the finite mode as substance-like. To be a mode of eternal substance is not to be oneself eternal in the way that substance is. Understanding a mode as eternal is rather a matter of understanding it in relation to substance, on which it depends. That dependence, we saw earlier, comes to each mode not directly from substance but mediated though the totality of other finite modes—its "external" causes, through which the sustaining force of substance is transmitted. So it depends on those external causes for its continued existence and thriving—a dependence that makes its eventual destruction inevitable.

The mind that comes to know itself and its ideas of other things as eternal understands that its dependence on external causes, which it grasped at the lowest level of knowledge, is also its relationship to eternal substance, whose mode it is. Such a mind knows its eternity in the midst of transience. Duration and eternity are reconciled in its existence, although, as ways of understanding that existence, they remain radically distinct.

The Intellectual Love of God

All modes are dependent on substance, without which they can neither be nor be conceived. All can be said to be eternal (IIP45; vP29S). What then is distinctive about the eternity of the mind? For Spinoza it is not the case that minds are a special kind of entity with an attribute of immortality that sets them apart from other things. Minds are not immune to the destructibility that afflicts the rest of nature. The Axiom of Part Four, that everything in nature is such that there is something more powerful which can destroy it, is clearly meant to apply to minds along with all other finite modes. What is distinctive about the mind is just that, unlike other modes, it can come to a realization of its own eternity. It can make a transition between the two ways of understanding a thing as actual. And what is particularly important is that it can make that transition with respect to its own self-understanding. It can pass from being the idea of a body understood durationally to being a more reflective idea of the basis of that duration.

The mind can come to an understanding of what is involved in its own status as mode of substance. This is what makes the difference between the virtuous mind and the mind that lacks virtue. The virtuous mind comes to understand the body of which it is the idea, and hence itself, "under a species of eternity" (vP29). Whereas the nonvirtuous mind lives as if it knew neither itself "nor God, nor things," the virtuous mind moves from the state of ignorance to the state of reflective awareness" (vP42S). However, this is a puzzling transformation. The mind, it seems, is supposed to transform itself into something that was there all along. How can the status of eternal mode be something that is acquired? The mind struggles to become something that is already there—the eternal essence of the body of which it is the idea.

Leibniz saw this as a problem in Spinoza's version of the eternity of the mind. If Spinoza is right, he says in a letter to Landgrave (14 August 1683), there would be no place for self-improvement in order to leave after us an eternal essence, for that essence would be already in nature, whether we try to resemble it or not. And how would it be any use to us after death, if we are no longer anything, to have resembled such an idea? Spinoza himself speaks of the transformation of the mind from the one state to the other as a fiction—as something we feign (vP31S, P33S). It is a useful fiction, he says, to think of the mind's eternity as something it acquires. This fiction is connected with another—the fiction of the intellectual joy with which God contemplates himself.

Joy involves a transition to a greater state of activity. Such transitions are inapplicable to God. He cannot pass to a greater or lesser perfection. So he is not really affected by joy or sadness. Strictly speaking, he loves no one and hates no one (vP17). We can nonetheless say that God loves himself with an infinite intellectual love. For he enjoys infinite perfection, accompanied by the idea of himself—that is, since he is self-caused, by the idea of his cause (vP35Dem). And, by Spinoza's definitions of love and joy, that is what intellectual love is. Although not strictly joy, this state has affinities with joy. It involves not the transition to greater perfection but perfection itself. Our intellectual love of God, which Spinoza identifies with intuitive knowledge, can likewise be treated as joy only through a kind of feigning, though one which is equally harmless, provided we know what we are doing. It is the same fiction whereby we treat the mind as able to become eternal. We consider the mind "as if it were now beginning to be, and were now beginning to understand things under a species of eternity" (vP31S).

In context, this is of course a complex exercise in fiction, for it coincides with what should be the real condition of attentive readers of the *Ethics*. The intellectual love of God, which arises from the third kind of knowledge, is eternal (vP33). But, although strictly it has had no beginning, it still has all the perfections of love, just as if it had, as we feigned, begun to be. "There is no difference here, except that the Mind has had eternally the same perfections which, in our fiction, now come to it, and that it is accompanied by the idea of God as an eternal cause. If Joy, then, consists in the passage to a greater perfection, blessedness must surely consist in the fact that the Mind is endowed with perfection itself" (vP33S). What is fictional is the idea that this love has come to be. This intellectual love of God is in fact the same as God's eternal love of himself—a love that does not result from a transition to a greater state of perfection but consists in perfection itself. "The Mind's intellectual Love of God is the very Love of God by which God loves himself" (vP36). Insofar as God loves himself, he loves human beings, and consequently God's love of us and the mind's intellectual love of God are one and the same. Our "salvation, or blessedness, or Freedom" consists in this "constant and eternal love of God" or—for it comes to the same thing—God's love for us. Whether it is related to God or to the mind, it can rightly be called "satisfaction of mind" (vP36S). It follows necessarily from the nature of the mind, so there is nothing that can take it away. Anything that could remove it would be "contrary to the true," which is absurd (vP37Dem).

The intellectual love of God thus follows naturally from reflection on what is involved in being a mode of thought—from the knowledge that the mind, with respect to both essence and existence, follows from the divine nature and continually depends on God (vP36S). Spinoza insists that the mind's eternity, like the knowledge of God involved in it, is really quite commonly known, although in both cases, under the influence of imagination, we think we do not have it, imagining it as quite different from what it is. "If we attend to the common opinion of men, we shall see that they are indeed conscious of the eternity of their Mind, but that they confuse it with duration, and attribute it to the imagination, or memory, which they believe remains after death" (vP34S).

Despite the identification of the mind's intellectual love of God and God's love of himself, there is of course a crucial contrast between the two forms of this love. It echoes Spinoza's discussion of the nature of the mind in Part Two. The mind's intellectual love of God is "part of the infinite Love by which God loves himself" (vP36). It is an action by which the mind contemplates itself, with an accompanying idea of God as cause. And it is hence "an action by which God, insofar as he can be explained through the human Mind, contemplates himself, with the accompanying idea of himself (as the cause)" (vP36Dem). It is the same love but with a crucial shift of focus. Spinoza relies on this shift to give his version of the eternity of the mind continuity with more traditional doctrines of immortality. Nothing—not even my ceasing to exist—can take away this intellectual love of God, whereby God eternally loves himself. But it is one and the same as my present intellectual love of God, my exercise of the third kind of knowledge. By a shift of focus, we can move from our present love of God to God's eternal love of himself, determined in this particular mode—a love to which the passage of time and our destructibility is of no consequence.

The Eternity of the Mind

Although Spinoza, unlike Descartes, regards the human mind as destructible, he also thinks that the mind's intellectual love of God is indestructible. These apparently inconsistent claims are supposed to be reconciled through the distinction between the two ways of understanding the mind as actual. The Axiom of Part Four, which insists that all singular things are destructible, concerns, he says, things only insofar as they are considered "in relation to a certain time and place"—only, then, in relation to one of the ways of understanding a thing as actual (vP37S). But this coexistence of an indestructible intellectual love of God with the destructibility of the mind that has it clearly does raise problems about the interpretation of Spinoza's doctrine of the eternity of the mind. It is difficult, to see how the doctrine can be taken as a version of immortality. Yet it is clear too that Spinoza means it to have some continuities with more traditional doctrines of an afterlife.

The eternity of the mind is supposed to reconcile us to death. After our death something, which can be identified with what is now our actual existence, will continue to be the case. But Spinoza seems not to think of this as the continued existence of a self. It is not surprising that commentators should give up in bewilderment in response to this strange conjunction of claims.[3] If Spinoza's eternity of the mind is not

3. Wolfson presents the doctrine of the eternity of the mind as a lapse into mysticism: Wolfson, *The Philosophy of Spinoza*, p. 350. A. E. Taylor refers to it as one of the incoherencies of Spinoza's thought: Alfred Taylor, "Some Incoherencies in Spinozism, Part II," *Mind* 46, 281–301, reprinted in S. Paul Kashap, ed., *Studies in Spinoza* (Berkeley: University of California Press, 1972). More recently, Jonathan Bennett has dismissed it as unsalvageable. After three centuries of failure to profit from Part Five, he suggests, "the time has come to admit that this part of the *Ethics* has nothing to teach us and is pretty certainly worthless": *A Study of Spinoza's Ethics* (Cambridge: Cambridge University Press, 1984), p. 372. A notable exception to this tendency to dismiss these sections of the *Ethics* is the excellent discussion of Spinoza's treatment of "Last Things" in Alan Donagan's *Spinoza* (Chicago: University of Chicago Press, 1989), pp. 190–207. Yirmiyahu Yovel also offers an interesting account of Spinoza's intuitive knowledge as a form of "secular salvation," consisting not in immortality but in the realization of eternity within time (chapter 6 of *Spinoza and Other Heretics*, vol. 1, "The Marrano of Reason" [Princeton: Princeton University Press, 1989], pp. 153–71). For a useful survey of earlier competing interpretations of Spinoza's doctrine of the eternity of the mind, see R. J. Delahunty, *Spinoza* (London: Routledge and Kegan Paul, 1985), chap. 9, pp. 279–305.

a doctrine of survival, is it not misleading for him to present it as continuous with earlier doctrines of immortality? But, although Spinoza's doctrine is at odds with the more familiar Cartesian doctrine, it does echo some earlier ways of thinking of immortality which Descartes's theory of the mind as an indestructible intellectual substance had left behind.

In his dedication of the *Meditations* to the faculty at the Sorbonne, Descartes claimed as a virtue of his philosophy its capacity to demonstrate the immortality of the soul. In the synopsis to the work he presents the proof as resting on the soul's indivisibility. We cannot conceive of half a mind, whereas we can always conceive of half a body, however small. This leads us to recognize the natures of mind and of body as not only different but in some ways opposites. The arguments he produces, he says, are sufficient to show that the decay of the body does not imply the destruction of the mind and are hence enough to give mortals the hope of an afterlife (AT vii, 13; Cott. ii, 10). Because the human mind is a substance, it must be by nature incorruptible and unable to cease to exist unless reduced to nothingness by God's denying his concurrence. Body, taken in the general sense, is a substance, so that it too never perishes. But the human body, insofar as it differs from other bodies, is simply made up of a certain configuration of limbs and of other "accidents" of this sort. Individual bodies have for Descartes a status similar to that of modes in Spinoza's system. The human mind, in contrast, is a pure substance. All the "accidents" of the mind can change, so that it has different objects of understanding, different desires or sensations; but it does not on that account become a different mind. Our minds remain the same throughout changes in thought, whereas a human body loses its identity merely as a result of change in the shape of some of its parts. It follows, Descartes thinks, that while the body can very easily perish, the mind is immortal by its very nature.

In treating individual minds as substances Descartes of course dissociated himself from traditional ideas of the soul as form of the body, lacking the status of substance. The idea of mind and body as related as form to matter readily accommodated the close union of mind and body in a human being. But that view had difficulty in accommodating the orthodox religious belief in the individual soul's survival of death. Hence Descartes's boast of his theory's consistency with religious doctrine. Spinoza's version of the mind's eternity is clearly not, as Descartes's was, a theory of the indestructibility of the individual mind. Nor is it a theory of intellectual immortality of the kind found in the Aristotelian tradition. Aristotle speaks in Book 12 of the Metaphysics of a divine thinking that is one with the object of its thought and indivisible throughout eternity. Since divine thought is the most excellent of things, he reasons, it must be of itself that it thinks, and its thought is a thinking on thinking. And in the *De Anima* he associates the active intellect with a kind of immortality. Arabic commentators developed these passages as a theory of the eternal existence of a unitary thinking thing—a conception of immortality that, as Aquinas pointed out in his treatise *On the Unity of the Intellect against the Averroists,* was irreconcilable with anything of the individual human soul surviving death and that hence could not allow for rewards and punishments.[4] Aquinas interpreted Aristotle's remarks on immortality and the active intellect as, instead, affirming the survival of the soul as form of the body, so far as its intellectual part is concerned. The survival of the intellect, he thinks, is made possible by the fact that, unlike the other powers of the soul, it does not have a corporeal organ. But the interim between individual bodily death and the general resurrection of the body was an embarrassment for a theory of soul that attempted to preserve the spirit of Aristotle's treatment of the soul as the form of the body. Individual immortality on Aristotelian lines was tenuous in both content and consistency.

In the *Short Treatise* Spinoza combined features of both Cartesian

4. St. Thomas Aquinas, *On the Unity of the Intellect against the Averroists,* trans. B. H. Zedler (Milwaukee: Marquette University Press, 1968), chap. 4, sec. 86, p. 59.

and pre-Cartesian treatments of immortality. There are references in that work to a "thinking thing" in which the individual soul exists as an idea. Intellect in this thinking thing is like motion in extension. It is "a Son, product or immediate creature of God, also created by him from all eternity, and remaining immutable to all eternity." Its sole property is to "understand everything clearly and distinctly at all times," from which arises immutably "a satisfaction infinite, or most perfect, since it cannot omit doing what it does" (Part I, chap. 9; G. 1/48; C. 92). The role of this thinking thing in the *Short Treatise* echoes Maimonides' version of the Active Intellect in the *Guide for the Perplexed*. Maimonides, following Arabic commentators on Aristotle, linked Aristotle's treatment of the union of the active intellect and its objects with the Aristotelian cosmology of the spheres. He presents the active intellect as a transcendent intelligence, the "last of the purely spiritual beings," an intelligence of the same kind as those that govern the movement of the spheres. Its origin is the intelligence that sets in motion the sphere nearest the earth. The active intellect puts human minds into act, in a way analogous to that in which the intelligences set their spheres in motion. The human mind, or at any rate part of it, attains immortality through its influence, coming to the state of knowledge which is the greatest human perfection and the source of eternal life.[5]

In his fragmentary and obscure treatment of the immortality of the soul in the *Short Treatise* (Part II, chap. 23), Spinoza brings this theme of immortality through contact with the "thinking thing" together with some more Cartesian themes of the soul's relations to God. In the *Short Treatise* the soul is an idea in the thinking thing. Its immortality comes from knowledge, described—in terms reminiscent of Descartes's treatment of love in the *Passions of the Soul*—as a union in which lover and loved form one whole. Spinoza, in the chapter on love

5. Maimonides, *Guide for the Perplexed*, trans. Michael Friedlander (New York: Dover, 1956), Part II, chap. 4; pp. 157–58.

in the *Short Treatise,* presents this feature of love as a source of wretchedness for the lover of transient things. Love is a union with an object that our intellect judges to be "good and magnificent"—a union that makes lover and loved become one and the same thing or form a whole together (Part II, chap. 5; G. 1/63; C. 105–106). So those who unite themselves with corruptible things are always miserable, for the objects of their love are outside their power and subject to many accidents. This relation of love or knowledge is also the basis of the *Short Treatise* account of mind-body union. The soul can be united either with the body of which it is the idea or with God, without whom it can neither exist nor be understood. If it is united with the body only and the body perishes, then the soul too must perish. For if it lacks the body, which is "the foundation of its love," the soul must perish with the body. But if the soul is united with another thing, which is and remains immutable, it will have to remain immutable also. So if the soul unites itself with God, who is imperishable, it too will be imperishable (G. 1/103; C. 141).

The *Short Treatise* contains many exhortations that we should concern ourselves with what is eternal, transcending transient things, to love what will not fail us. Here the soul is not of its nature imperishable. But it can become so through the right choice of love objects—a choice grounded in adequate knowledge of its dependence on God. Because the first thing the soul comes to know is the body, it is united to the body in love. But, because every love is destroyed when we perceive something better, it follows that, if we come to know God as clearly as we know our own body, we must come to be more closely united with him than with it, being released, as it were, from the body (Part II, chap. 19; G. 1/93/3; C. 133).

Since love cannot withstand the confrontation with something it regards as better than what it already has, the pursuit of transient objects of affection is always fraught with misery. No transient thing can retain a steady hold on our affections. We abandon what we come to see as inferior. But reason shows that all things depend on and hence are inferior to God, without whom they cannot be understood. Reason directs us to part from such transitory things and leads us to the love of God, which saves us from falling into the "bog of the passions." Since the love of God is an unlimited love, it can always increase, becoming ever more excellent from its union with an infinite object (Part II, chap. 14; G. I, 78; C. 119).

Love, Spinoza suggests in the *Short Treatise,* is essential to human existence. In passages reminiscent of Descartes's treatment of thought in the Second Meditation, Spinoza suggests that if we ceased to love we would cease to exist. We cannot even seek to be free of love, any more than we could seek to be released from the demands of Cartesian consciousness. If we knew nothing, we would also be nothing. "So it is necessary that we not be free of it, because, given the weakness of our nature, we could not exist if we did not enjoy something to which we were united, and by which we were strengthened" (Part II, chap. 5; G. 1/62; C. 105). The shift from love of our bodies to love of God echoes Descartes's transition, in the Meditations, from self-knowledge to knowledge of God, on whom our being depends. We come to know God better than we know ourselves, Spinoza says, because without him we cannot know ourselves at all (Part II, chap. 19; G. 1/93/3; C. 133). We must love and unite with something. But union with transient things does not strengthen our own nature. "For they are weak, and the one cripple cannot support the other" (Part II, chap. 5; G. 1/63; C. 105). Our minds are ideas of our bodies, but cannot find rest in that awareness. So we pass over into knowledge of that without which neither body nor idea of it can exist or be understood. This transition is a "second birth," in which we move to the love of God, as different from the love of the body as spirit is from flesh. This love and union give rise to "an eternal and immutable constancy" (Part II, chap. 22; G. 1/102; C. 140).

In the *Ethics* Spinoza combines these various themes from earlier approaches to immortality, transforming them into a distinctive form of reconciliation to death. Maimonides' "thinking thing" is echoed in

Spinoza's "mind of God." However, it is no longer a transcendent intelligence but rather the expression of substance under the attribute of thought. The individual human mind is an idea in this mind of God, with body as its object. It can no longer choose to attach itself to God in any way that releases it from its status as idea of the body. But it can come to understand that body and, hence, itself in relation to the idea of God. It can become more fully aware of its status as an idea in the mind of God—an idea in the interconnected totality of thought, loving in an eternal intellectual love the substance of which it is a mode. This eternal love does not give it access to any transcendent thinking thing that escapes the onslaught of time and contingency. The mind, like the body of which it is the idea, remains destructible. But it knows itself as part of God's eternal self-love. It knows that its love of God is the same as that whereby God eternally loves himself, although the self-love of substance is determined in an infinite multiplicity of other modes as well.

The Cartesian themes of the *Short Treatise* are also transformed in the *Ethics*. Indivisibility is no longer a distinctive mark of minds, but a feature of the *conatus*, which is essential to both minds and bodies. The unity of a body, consisting in the preservation of its distinctive proportions of motion to rest, can survive the loss or replacement of component parts. And the unity of the mind comes from its being the idea of that bodily unity, although, as we have seen, it has its own *conatus* as the active articulation of bodily awareness. Although it cannot release itself from body, it can release itself from the passive awareness that is the bondage of passion. Minds, no less than bodies, are modes of substance and parts of a whole. They differ from bodies not in lacking complexity but in their capacity to come to understand their relations to, and dependence on, the whole. They differ from bodies, in other words, in their capacity for self-knowledge.

Spinoza also transforms the Cartesian relations between self-knowledge and the knowledge of God. Self-knowledge is the reflective awareness of body. In knowing our bodies, we know ourselves.

But in coming to that knowledge what we know and love is not a transient and perishable thing that will bring us, against our proper nature, to share in its destructibility, like one cripple leading another, in the phrase Spinoza uses in the *Short Treatise*. Rather, in knowing ourselves, we come to a knowledge and love of substance, whose modes we are. The shift to love of God is here not a shedding of an inferior object of love but rather a shift of focus within the act of understanding. Descartes's idea of love as willingly forming a union, a whole with something, is transformed into the idea of an intellectual understanding of our status as parts of a unified whole.

Spinoza's Account of Death

Intuitive knowledge is supposed to engage with our actual existence in a powerfully affective way, yielding an understanding of ourselves as eternal. What then is supposed to happen when such a mind ceases to exist? Has Spinoza given us a vision of our eternity only to render our deaths incomprehensible? What, we may ask, is the difference between the inclusion of a mind, during life, in the totality of thought and its inclusion, after death, in that same totality? With respect to the totality, it may make no difference at all. And this indeed seems to be the basis for Spinoza's version of the mind's eternity. But from the perspective of the individual mind, the difference seems quite radical. As an idea of an actually existing body, my mind exists only while that body exists. To know that my existence will have been part of the totality of being may seem small comfort to a mind doomed to lose its consciousness of that very fact, along with all else. What then is the difference between the mind as it exists during life and the same mind as it continues to be contained in the totality of thought after death? What is it that the mind loses at death?

It seems clear that Spinoza thinks that at death the mind loses all possibility of awareness of actual existence. "The mind can neither imagine anything, nor recollect past things, except while the Body endures" (vP21). But not only does it not remember or imagine after death, it does not even "endure." Our mind, we are told, can be said to endure only insofar as it involves the actual existence of the body (vP23S). If we take seriously Spinoza's denial of both consciousness and duration to the mind after death, there seems no way we can allow for any continued perception of the totality from different perspectives. For perspectives are provided by our actually existing bodies, impinging on, and impinged on by, others.

We seem to have here a bewildering array of apparently inconsistent claims. We know, from the Axiom of Part Four, that nothing indestructible exists in nature. And we know that we are indeed part of nature. Yet we also "feel and know by experience" that we are eternal (vP23S). Spinoza even explicitly claims that the human mind cannot be absolutely destroyed with the body, that something of it "remains," which is eternal (vP23). So the claim is not that the wise mind finds within itself some privileged invulnerability to change and decay, which does not apply to the rest of nature. It feels and knows that it is eternal despite, and indeed because of, the dependent, modal status it shares with all other finite things. So what "remains" cannot be something that endures after death. Not only does the mind not retain any continuity of consciousness with what existed during life, it seems it cannot even be said to continue to exist through time.

Some commentators have tried to salvage Spinoza's eternity of the mind as a coherent account of the survival of the human soul, or at any rate part of it. Alan Donagan, in an ingenious attempt in this direction, talks of Spinoza's eternal essence as part of an actually existing individual. So the thing as a complex, including that essence, can be said to perish, while the essence itself exists at all times.[6] But such talk

6. Alan Donagan, "Spinoza's Proof of Immortality," in Marjorie Grene, ed., *Spinoza: A Collection of Critical Essays* (New York: Anchor Press/Doubleday, 1973), pp. 241–48. See also, in the same volume, pp. 227–40, Martha Kneale, "Eternity and Sempiternity," originally published in *Proceedings of the Aristotelian Society*, vol. 69, pp. 223–38. Donagan further discusses the bearing of Spinoza's treatment of essence on the eternity of the mind in the final chapter of his *Spinoza*.

of the omnitemporality of an essence seems to conflict with both Spinoza's strong resistance to separating essence from the existence of the thing and his resistance to thinking of eternity in terms of a prolongation of existence.

What then can we say is left of the mind after death? Nothing, it seems, but the truth of all that has been—a truth grasped, if at all, only from the standpoint of the whole. But should not that mean that nothing remains of the individuality of the mind? It is useful here to contrast Spinoza's treatment of the eternity of the mind with his treatment of the nonexistence of fictional entities. Let us come back to his example in Part Two of the boy imagining the winged horse. If he takes the image for a real horse, rather than a mere bodily trace, his bodily modifications form, as it were, a false whole, in which traces of past modifications are conjoined with present ones. The imagining of the winged horse can be seen as a complex of temporally disparate modes, lacking the unity of a true individual. To have such an awareness without error, the boy's mind must encompass it in a wider whole, in which its inadequacy is manifested or in which it is "excluded from existence."[7] In those wider wholes inadequacy can be accommodated or neutralized. The mind's limited position in the totality of thought, as we saw earlier, makes it impossible for it to perceive all finite modes as thus part of wider wholes. And its perception of its own body poses special problems. The mind can perceive subsets of its own bodily modifications as parts of wholes, but it cannot perceive the body of which it is the idea as excluded from existence in wider wholes. If the collective force of encompassing modes excludes the body from existence, the mind will cease to perceive actual bodily modifications and hence cease to exist. The nonexistence of the body involves the mind's own nonexistence, and this the mind cannot itself affirm.

For Descartes the impossibility of affirming our nonexistence involved the mind's realization of its independence and invulnerability

7. For an illuminating discussion of Spinoza's description of images as "excluding" one another, see Donagan, *Spinoza*, pp. 47–49.

as a thinking thing. For Spinoza it involves, rather, a realization of its dependence on other modes of thought—its status as part of a whole. The mind cannot perceive the wholes in which its own nonexistence can be accommodated. But it can, through reason, come to understand that it is indeed thus contained. The mind can come to understand itself, truly, as lacking the self-contained character of substance and hence as needing to form wholes with other things in order to exist—wholes that can sustain and enrich it, but which also render it inherently destructible. The individual mind cannot encompass within itself the sources of its own destruction. But it can know that there are external causes—rival *conatus* that will destroy it.

The winged horse is a fiction, whereas the mind, though also accommodated into wider wholes, is actual. The mind has a unified *conatus* of its own, whereas the imagined winged horse is just a succession of modes, improperly conjoined—an artificial unity, with no power to draw strength from congenial *conatus* or to fight back against rival ones. The traces that make up its false unity are accommodated within the wider totality that is the boy's mind—rendered consistent with the truth, without being thereby denied existence. The winged horse is neither a real individual nor a single image or trace. In imagining it, the boy is aware of a set of modifications of his body, patterned in relation to other modifications. But there is here no unified *conatus* exerting causal force in the world. Fictions can stand in some kinds of causal relations to nonfictional things. The winged horse as an intentional object—a constituent of the boy's imaginative life—may have effects on him and, through him, on others. It is a real pattern, part of the totality of a mind, but it lacks the true unity of *conatus*.

Death is the destruction of *conatus*. In this respect the mind that has ceased to exist resembles the winged horse. It cannot engage in that mixed resistance and enjoyment of conative interaction that is life. The basic form of the mind's struggle is for self-knowledge, and to the extent that it does understand itself it sees itself increasingly as part of nature. The understanding of itself as eternal is the other side of the coin to this understanding of itself as part of nature—transient, vulnerable, and inevitably to be destroyed. But death does not reduce it to the status of a fiction. Death has no power to make it not have been. The mind that has ceased to exist lacks *conatus*. It may continue to have effects in the world, through the interconnections it formed in life, but it no longer strives or struggles in its own right. Since for Spinoza that striving to persist, in conflict and collaboration with other things, was its essence, there is a sense in which its essence is gone. Yet Spinoza also insists that its essence is eternal. What can we make of this?

Spinoza talks of the idea that is the human mind being excluded from existence by other ideas (iiiPiiS). The example of the imagined winged horse makes it clear that to be excluded from existence by wider encompassing ideas is not to be annihilated, but rather to be accommodated into wider wholes. False unities that lack *conatus* are accommodated into living *conatus*. There is a way in which this process is paralleled in the case of the mind that ceases to exist. The traces of past modifications that make up the boy's image are part of a living totality that is his mind—the idea of a unified body undergoing present changes and preserving past ones. And the idea of that unified body is in turn accommodated into wider wholes, totalities that will accommodate the idea of his body after it has ceased to be itself a living center of struggle, pain, and joy.

It may be tempting here to construe this accommodation into wider wholes as a matter of the dead living on in the memory and imagination of the living. This does give us something analogous to the insertion of the 'idea' of the winged horse into the wider totality that is the boy's mind, in which it is negated without being annihilated. To negate the existence of the winged horse is not to deny the reality of the set of modifications that make up the fiction. It is to deny that fiction the status of a unified idea, to which something must correspond under the attribute of extension. The 'idea' finds its place in the

wider whole that is the boy's mind without being asserted as truth. It is
not articulated as itself a unified whole. This fictional 'idea' is not, of
itself, a unified affirmation. It can be affirmed only as included in a
wider whole. The mind that has ceased to exist can be seen as having
this kind of existence in the ideas of others, just as it had it in life. But
Spinoza means by the eternity of the mind something more than this
relatively straightforward form of survival. The eternity of the mind is
not just a matter of our surviving in the memories and imagination of
others. The words of the dead may, as Auden put it in his poem on the
death of Yeats, be scattered in the guts of the living. But nothing can
take away their own completeness and individuality, and this is what
Spinoza tries to capture. The mind that has ceased to exist is for him
not just an image, or set of images, in the minds of others. The idea of
Peter's body which is identified with Peter's mind is a different idea
from those involved in other peoples' ideas of Peter's body, which
persist even though Peter does not exist (11P17S). It is my own idea of
my body—that idea which can be identified with my mind—which
Spinoza speaks of as becoming eternal.

The mind that has ceased to exist is an articulated whole, accommodated into the mind of God in a way that preserves its own wholeness and integrity. The mind of God is the totality of thought in which
all true individuals exist in a network of interconnected wholes. The
'idea' of the winged horse occurs in that totality only as a subsidiary
formation in the boy's mind. It has no articulated place of its own in
the totality. The jigsaw analogy, despite its limitations as a way of
understanding Spinoza's theory of error, is of some use here. The
winged horse figures in the whole only as part of the pattern on a piece
of the jigsaw—not as a piece that could be independently slotted into
the totality. But the idea of myself that is the bearer of my mind's
eternity is not the idea of me which lives in the minds of others,
reflecting the ways in which the ideas of my bodily modifications in
life are interconnected with their continuing ideas of their own bodily
modifications. As a unity, the mind retains an articulated place in the

totality, of a kind the idea of the winged horse lacks. The mind retains its own integrity, a wholeness, despite its insertion into wider wholes. It is not reduced to mere fragmentation, to be given unity only in the living perception of others.

Having seen what it is not, what can we say of Spinoza's version of the eternity of the mind? Part of it is the idea that the individuality of the living is not affected by death. Death does not transform us into fictions. We have seen earlier that Spinoza does not see individuality as an illusion depending on a subjective view of the world. The view of the whole is not for him a perception in which the individuality of minds is eclipsed. So to say that the Spinozistic mind remains is not to say that at death its individuality disappears back into an undifferentiated whole. He speaks in Part Two of a kind of existence that modes have "in the attributes"—an existence that finds inadequate illustration in the undifferentiated existence of unspecified rectangles in a circle (11P8S). This passage, obscure though it is, does seem to indicate that Spinoza thinks that there is no differentiation of ideas of what never exists, any more than the nonexistent essences themselves are separated out as identifiable individuals that happen not to exist. To cease to exist is not like having never existed. For Spinoza, it is only actual existence that yields discrete individuals.[8]

But in trying to understand death we are dealing with the nonexistence of a specific individual, a determinate finite thing that did exist in the past. It does not exist only as "contained in the attributes." Substance is eternally realized in the individuals we are. Neither our individuality nor our eternity is fictional. Death destroys *conatus*, ending that endeavor to persist in being in which our individuality has

---

8. For an interesting and challenging alternative reading of Spinoza's discussion of ideas of nonexistent objects see Donagan's *Spinoza*, pp. 194–97. On Donagan's reading, the ideas of the nonexistent rectangles have an actuality for which there is no correlate under the attribute of extension, although, as he acknowledges, this is at first sight inconsistent with the parallelism between the order of ideas and that of things.

resided. But there is an eternal "mind"—an all-encompassing "idea"—into which our living selves are accommodated in a way that resists the ravages of time and death. And we can during life come to realize this truth. It is a truth that inevitably we fictionalize—as if it were a stage to be reached beyond death, something beyond life. But this is a very different kind of fiction from that involved in the imagining of the winged horse. The truth beneath the fiction is that there is during life something that transcends life and time. And we can grasp it during life, though we cannot grasp it, or indeed anything, after death. But the content of the perception is such that once we have it, death becomes of little consequence.

If the idea that we become eternal is a conscious "fiction," what is the truth that this exercise in feigning is supposed to help us grasp? It centers on the essence of the mind. And this, as we have seen, is something that is not detachable from existence. The truth of the mind's eternity is something to be grasped from within actual existence—something to be understood during life. For after life there is no memory, no imagination. For Aquinas, and—for different reasons—for Descartes, that lack would not have prevented intellect from functioning. But for Spinoza the higher forms of thought are much more firmly anchored in memory and imagination. This is part of the reason why the mind's becoming eternal is a fiction. We think of it as a change that happens at death. But in truth it is something that is true now. Because our thought is not merely anchored in imagination but blinkered by it, we think of the mind's eternity as a persistence after death. But this, Spinoza insists, is an error. Eternity is not to be construed in terms of the continuation of existence.

What then is the content of the perception we are supposed to have during life of the mind's eternity? And if it is indeed true that it is something that must be perceived during life—because after death the mind can perceive nothing—is not that to say that it is an illusion? It may seem that what Spinoza is offering is an imagined eternity, a delusion that could be known to be such only at death. But if it is a delusion, of course, it will not be known to be such even then, since there will be no mind to grasp it. Spinoza's eternity of the mind may seem to offer an understanding, which can be grasped only during life, of what lies beyond death. But if this seems paradoxical it is a paradox that is in the nature of the question. To think of the mind as experiencing oblivion after death is just as much an illusion as to think of it as experiencing joy or pain. If it is illusion to think that our joys will continue after death, it is just as much an illusion to think that the hopeful mind might discover at death, to its disappointment, that nothing awaits it. We have here, not an inconsistency, but a deep insight that underlies Spinoza's talk of the becoming eternal of the mind as a "fiction," through which we glimpse the truth.

The Spinozistic mind aspires to understand itself as an integral part in a total unified articulation of the world, sustained by the necessary being of substance. It is the mind's recognition that it has such a place in a systematically unified order of thought that sustains the full Spinozistic reconciliation to finitude. What is supposed to reconcile us to death is the perception of the mind as part of a systematically interconnected totality of thought, a unified "idea." And its reconciling power has to do with Spinoza's understanding of both individuality and time. The mind of God, of which the individual mind comes to see itself as part, is the total articulation in thought of all that there at any time is. It is not a totality of omnitemporal ideas; each constituent idea ceases to exist, along with its correlated finite mode of extension. The eternal intellect of God is more appropriately seen as the totality of all that is ever true than as a totality of omnitemporal truths. However, such a totality does in a sense transcend time. The character of what is past is not altered by the passage of time. This is not to deny that there are important differences between present, past, and future. But that an event is over, or that a thing has ceased to be, does not intrude on what it has been. This aspect of the "eternity" of finite modes derives from the relationship between truth and time. It can be expressed without reference to truth as a unified totality.

That is the aspect of the eternity of the mind stressed in Santayana's exposition of the doctrine. "A man who understands himself under the form of eternity knows the quality that eternally belongs to him, and knows that he cannot wholly die, even if he would; for when the movement of his life is over, the truth of his life remains."[9] The point is also captured in Timothy Sprigge's formulation: "Facts are not subject to change though not because they are prolonged through time. They cannot somehow be blotted out from reality and cease to be."[10] But the full Spinozistic reconciliation to mortality depends on an idea that must be more problematical for modern minds—the idea of a systematically interconnected "whole of nature," in which things past, present, and future are unified by reciprocal dependencies, mediating the causal force of the one substance. The Spinozistic mind aspires to understand itself as an integral part in a total, unified articulation of the world, sustained by the necessary being of substance. It is the mind's recognition that it has such a place in a systematically unified order of thought that is supposed to make death of no consequence. It is not just our having existed, but *what* we are, that is bound up with other things existing before and after us. So the mind's being is not circumscribed by its existence as idea of actually existing body. Not only is it the case that we are included in the totality of what has been; it is also true that what we are is interdependent with other finite modes that exist when we do not. So the doctrine of the necessary interconnections of modes—if we could believe it—would give us a stake in the future that goes beyond our merely being now something that will continue to have been.

Individuality and Death

The content I have so far given to Spinoza's talk of the eternity of the mind is accessible to reason. Should we expect some special, additional content for his intuitive knowledge? To search for an utterly

9. George Santayana, Introduction to Spinoza's *Ethics*, trans. Andrew Boyle (London: Everyman/Dent, 1910), pp. xviii–xix.

10. Timothy Sprigge, "Ideal Immortality," *Southern Journal of Philosophy* (Summer 1972), 219–36.

new content of the intuitive perception which supposedly yields eternity of the mind would, I think, be to misunderstand how it relates to the lower kinds of knowledge. Perhaps we are now in a position to better see just how the third kind of knowledge is supposed to go beyond the second, and how it better reflects Spinoza's version of the relations between essence and existence.

Intuitive knowledge understands things as actually existing in relation to substance, in a way that eludes reason's understanding of things through common notions. That singular finite things depend on substance is of course a truth that does not wait upon the highest kind of knowledge. Spinoza has already demonstrated it through reason before he moves on to consider it, in Part Five, in relation to intuitive knowledge. What is distinctive about intuitive knowledge is that it can grasp this truth with reference to a particular case. When this happens, Spinoza tells us, it affects the mind much more powerfully than the general truth can. Intuitive knowledge of singular things is much more powerful than the "universal" knowledge that he has called knowledge of the second kind. "Although I have shown generally in Part One that all things (and consequently the human Mind also) depend on God both for their essence and their existence; nevertheless, that demonstration, though legitimate and put beyond all chance of doubt, still does not affect our Mind as much as when this is inferred from the very essence of any singular thing which we say depends on God" (vP36S). Its effects are especially powerful when this form of knowledge is brought to bear explicitly on knowledge of the singular things that we ourselves are—where we know ourselves by intuitive knowledge.

The third kind of knowledge has special connections with mortality, and this is related to its access to the understanding of individuality. The point can be illustrated through Tolstoy's remarkable evocation of the realization of mortality in "The Death of Ivan Ilyich":

> Ivan Ilyich saw that he was dying, and he was in continual despair.

In the depths of his heart he knew he was dying but, so far from growing used to the idea, he simply did not and could not grasp it.

The example of a syllogism which he had learned in Kiesewetter's *Logic:* Caius is a man, men are mortal, therefore Caius is mortal, had seemed to him all his life to be true as applied to Caius but certainly not as regards himself. That Caius—man in the abstract— was mortal, was perfectly correct; but he was not Caius, nor man in the abstract: he had always been a creature quite, quite different from all others . . . with all the joys and griefs and ecstasies of childhood, boyhood and youth . . .

And Caius was certainly mortal, and it was right for him to die; but for me, little Vanya, Ivan Ilyich, with all my thoughts and emotions—it's a different matter altogether. It cannot be that I ought to die. That would be too terrible.[11]

If he had to die, like Caius, surely, he thinks, he should have known. An inner voice would have told him so, but there was nothing of the sort. He and all his friends had felt that their case was quite different from Caius's. " 'And now here it is!' he said to himself. 'It can't—it can't be, and yet it is!' " Try as he may to drive the morbid thought away, the thought, and the reality itself, come to confront him.

Ivan understands the general truth that all men are mortal. And since he knows that he is a man, he understands also that he himself falls under this general law. He knows that he is mortal in the way that he knows Caius will die. Yet in another and very real way, it is nonetheless true that he does not know it. He is now on the brink of the painful realization of something he has not previously known. But his lack of knowledge is not a defect in reason. It is not as if he falsely believes himself to be an exception to the general truth of mortality. The knowledge he has lacked, and which is now painfully impinging on him, is something that engages with his self-knowledge, with the

11. Leo Tolstoy, *"The Death of Ivan Ilyich" and Other Stories,* trans. Rosemary Edmonds (London: Penguin, 1960), pp. 137–38.

direct awareness of his individuality. It is an awareness of individuals, not just as falling under general rules or concepts accessible through reason, but as actually existing.

Knowledge of the third kind engages with the actual existence of individuals, and especially of ourselves, in a way that eludes mere reason. This coming together of reason and affectivity in intuition is for Spinoza the highest achievement of self-knowledge. But what it grasps is really just the old truth of the dependence of modes on substance, understood now, however, in a new way. It is the same kind of shift in perspective that was involved in realizing that the love with which we love God is the same as that by which he loves himself. Here the shift is in the understanding of the relationship between the particular and the general. The self comes to understand its own status as a mode of substance—to understand that it is a realization of God's eternal self-love. In intuitive knowledge we come to see ourselves in relation to the truths of individuality. We come to understand ourselves as transient expressions of substance, which is equally realized in a multitude of other individuals, through which our existence is mediated. The insight comes especially from the confrontation with death. It is in really knowing that we must die that we know that we are eternal. It is in knowing our transience that we truly know ourselves.

Hegel and Spinoza

Hegel, we saw earlier, regarded Spinoza's version of substance as rigid and unyielding, falling short of the full self-consciousness of spirit—a reality in which we cannot be at home with ourselves. It was, he thought, a static substance that did not actively realize itself in determinate forms—a substance that did not incorporate the dynamic movement of life. Self-consciousness and the awareness of life belong together for Hegel, and Spinoza's philosophy, he thinks, does justice to neither. But his own insights into the connections between self-consciousness, individuality, life, and death, have their beginnings—as he himself acknowledges in his *Lectures on the History of Philosophy*—in Spinoza.[12] And his development of these themes from their Spinozistic origins, although it is in some respects very different from the spirit of Spinoza's reconciliation to mortality, can help us see more clearly why Spinoza should have thought that the fullest achievement of self-consciousness comes out of the awareness of death.

Self-awareness and the awareness of life have for Hegel a common structure, and it is similar to Spinoza's treatment of the relations between substance and finite modes. In the *Shorter Logic*[13] Hegel says that this structure is implicit in inanimate things, becomes more explicit in living things, and is yet more explicit in self-consciousness. At its most basic level, the structure is just a matter of individual things falling under concepts—of the coming together of the particular and the universal. The understanding of life and self-consciousness articulates this implicit presence of the universal in the particular, bringing out the fact that the relationship between individual and universal is not an external one. The universal exists as the individual's own inward nature, not as an "abstract representation" brought to bear on it. Finite things thus combine individuality and universality. The individual is opposed to the universal, yet the universal is also its very self. And this for Hegel means that finite things are in a state of contradiction. This internal structure of finite things is seen more clearly in living things, which manifest their internal contradiction in death. Death liberates the universal from merely individual existence. The "kind"—the essential and universal part of the individual—liberates itself from individuality. This means that death is not to be seen

12. For an interesting discussion of Hegel's development of Spinoza's concept of substance in his own version of the absolute, see Yirmiyahu Yovel, *Spinoza and Other Heretics*, vol. 2, *The Adventures of Immanence* (Princeton: Princeton University Press, 1989), pp. 27–50.
13. References are to Hegel's *Shorter Logic*, trans. William Wallace (Oxford: Oxford University Press, 1904).

as an external intrusion on the reality of the individual, but as essential to it. The limitations of the finite do not merely come from outside. The finite, being radically self-contradictory, involves its own self-suppression. Life involves the germ of death (p. 148).

This may seem a very different way of thinking of death from Spinoza's idea of it as coming always from outside the individual—beyond its essence, beyond the *conatus* by which it strives to persist in being. But it can be seen as a development of his idea that to understand a thing as a mode of substance involves understanding the inevitability of its ceasing to exist. For Spinoza this is because its existence is mediated through the collective force of other finite things. It involves the idea that substance, expressed in this finite mode, is expressed in a multiplicity of others as well, without which this one would be unable to exist. This aspect of the dependence of Spinoza's finite modes on substance is echoed in Hegel's treatment of the relation between the individual and its kind. What the thing is—for him its "kind"—is not something that is confined to this individual only. In the case of living things, the inner contradiction between the thing and its kind—the relation of opposition within identity—becomes explicit. Life must be embodied in individual living things, but cannot rest there. The living being dies because it is a contradiction—between the universal kind, which it implicitly is, and immediate existence as an individual. But individual death is transcended in the continuation of the species.

For animal species, the immediacy of individual existence is overcome only by the "liberation" of the kind through death (p. 52). But human beings can achieve this overcoming of immediacy in a richer and more intensive way through knowledge. For merely "natural" individuals, the universal is "released" only by death. For human beings, knowledge achieves less drastically the same result, breaking the "bonds of individualism" that fetter nature in every part (p. 57). The contradiction in finite things, between individuality and universality, is the source of their mortality. Self-conscious beings experience this not just as a contradiction in objects of knowledge, but as an acute tension within themselves as knowers—a contradiction that is resolved by moving beyond the individualism of nature into universality.

Although Hegel sees knowledge as in this way surpassing the "defect of life," he also thinks that it can be in its own way equally one-sided, in the opposite direction, fostering an escape from the bonds of individualism into a universality that is only abstractly conceived. Human consciousness is for Hegel uneasily poised between two kinds of failure to apprehend the truth—the failure to overcome immediacy and the equally erroneous flight to a merely abstract universality. It is the risk of an abstract universality, ignoring its ties with the individual, that he sees exemplified in Spinoza. What keeps Spinozism at the level of abstract universality, according to Hegel, is the failure to include the concept of life in his treatment of substance. In Hegel's own account, it is the confrontation with death that brings the aware-ness of life as not exhausted by the determinate particular modes it takes on.

In his famous description of the master-slave struggle in the sec-tions on the truth of self-certainty of the *Phenomenology of Spirit,* the fear of death is presented as shaking everything stable in consciousness to its foundations, producing the transition to the freedom of self-consciousness. This new awareness of life has in fact the same struc-ture as self-consciousness. Both involve the emergence of the universal from mere immediacy. The sense of death brings awareness of life as not exhausted by any of the determinate particular modes it takes on. And Hegel's "ego" stands to its determinate objects of conscious-ness as life does to its particular modes. But from the perspective of self-consciousness, this common structure undergoes a reversal. The fear of death makes us aware of ourselves as but transient "vanish-ing moments" in which life is for a time embodied. But the self-consciousness that comes out of the experience reverses the relation-ships between the universal and the individual. In self-consciousness I am aware of myself as ego, encompassing the vanishing moments, just as life encompasses and transcends the vanishing moments that we ourselves are, as natural, mortal individuals. I am no longer the vanishing moment, about to be replaced by other embodiments of life. I now stand, rather, in the all-encompassing position of life.[14] It is a similar reversal to the one we have seen in Spinoza, between God's love of himself and the individual self's love of God. The same relation takes on different significance according to which term we take as starting point.

Hegel thus emphasizes the lack of self-consciousness and life in Spinoza's version of substance. But there are, as he himself acknowledges, strong echoes of the relations between substance and modes in his own treatment of the structure of self-consciousness and life. The beginnings of the Hegelian perception of the connections between self-consciousness and mortality are in Spinoza's treatment of what is involved in being a mode of substance. And there are strong echoes of Spinoza's treatment of the role of affectivity in self-consciousness in Hegel's story of the emergence of self-consciousness. Hegel's treatment of the "one-sidedness" of Spinoza's abstract universality does less than justice to Spinoza's return to the individual in intuitive knowledge, which is closer to the spirit of Hegel's own treatment of the universal than he allows.

There are nonetheless some important differences between Hegelian and Spinozistic self-consciousness. And they emerge strikingly in the imagery of mastery and dominance which proliferates in Hegel's treatment of knowledge as overcoming the immediacy of individualism. Hegel endorses, and reinforces, the connotations of dominance in Kant's treatment of knowledge. Knowledge involves a struggle with nature, which mirrors that whereby living things assimilate it in order to sustain life—a relation of mastery. Human knowledge likewise

14. My discussion of this aspect of the master-slave struggle owes much to Hans-Georg Gadamer's paper, "Hegel's Dialectic of Self-Consciousness," in *Hegel's Dialectic: Five Hermeneutical Studies*, trans. P. Christopher Smith (New Haven: Yale University Press, 1976), pp. 54–74.

struggles to overcome and assimilate what is other, to "appropriate and subdue" it to the self. "To this end the positive reality of the world must be as it were crushed and pounded, in other words idealised" (*Shorter Logic,* p. 88). The "I" as knower is the "crucible and fire" that consumes the loose plurality of sense and reduces it to unity. Its role in bringing objects of consciousness into unity is presented by Hegel as an exercise in the mastery of universality over individuality.

The drive of self-consciousness to mastery is at the same time a drive toward universality of consciousness, toward a transcending of what differentiates us as individual human beings, although Hegel presents this as a transition to a higher kind of individuality. As knowers, we attain to our true status as individuals only to the extent that we come to see ourselves as "universal" thinkers. To be a self-conscious individual is something very different from being a merely "natural" one. It involves personhood, to which we attain by being "permeated by universality." This is Hegel's version of the overcoming of finitude. Although self-conscious individuals remain subject to mortality, they do, in a sense, transcend death, along with the immediacy of the merely natural. Self-consciousness attains to a kind of individuality that is no longer at odds with universality. In rising above mere nature, consciousness breaks away from one kind of individuality into another. This higher individuality comes out of the fear of death. But, once there, death supposedly loses its threatening aspect and takes on a new significance. As natural beings we are threatened with annihilation by death. But, as spirit, it is we who "crush and pound," appropriate and subdue, so that the objective world is divested of its strangeness and we find ourselves at home in it.

Hegelian self-consciousness takes on a sublime equanimity in the face of death. Spirit achieves an exalted form of individuality by being shaken out of all that binds it to attachment to the "merely natural." It thus comes to be "at home with itself," in eternal imperishability. For Spinoza too fullness of self-consciousness is supposed to yield freedom and reconciliation to death. But for him it comes from a clear-sighted awareness of ourselves as part of nature. A Spinozistic mind, confronting the world through the body of which it is the idea, does not, as the Hegelian ego does, recognize the world as itself. Mind takes its content from the world, but the independence of the attributes makes images of appropriation and mastery inappropriate for Spinoza's view of knowledge. Hegel of course sees this lack of self-recognition in the world as a limitation. The freedom of Hegelian egos derives from transcendence of nature, although his version of this is different from Descartes's picture of mind's transcendence of body. Spinoza's version of self-consciousness remains outside the tradition of transcendence. We will see in the next chapter that this does not prevent it from affirming the dominance of human beings over the rest of nature. But, in the lack of the idea of transcendence, Spinoza's versions of both dominance and difference have very different connotations from the Cartesian model.

FIVE

O

Dominance and Difference

Human beings, as has often been remarked, occupy an ambivalent position in nature, an ambivalence that philosophers have tried to resolve by an emphasis on—even an exultation in—the distinctive human capacity for knowledge. We may, as Pascal summed it up in his *Thoughts*, be the weakest reeds in nature. But we are thinking reeds.[1] Poised though we are between the two abysses of nothingness and infinity, we can draw comfort from the fact that, even though it may need only a drop of vapor to kill us, we are still nobler than the whole universe. For we know that we are dying and the advantage the universe has over us, of all of which the universe knows nothing. We may be unable to know nature in its infinite extent. We do not know it all, but that we know at all makes us superior to the rest of nature, which is not only ultimately unknowable but unknowing.

Pascal's theme of our superiority as knowers over the rest of nature reverberates through modern philosophy. For him the ambivalence of our position in nature is only ambivalently resolved through our self-esteem as knowers. Nature is, after all, unknowable as well as unknow-

---

1. Blaise Pascal, *Thoughts*, fragment 347 of Brunschvicg ed., trans. Alban J. Krailsheimer (Harmondsworth: Penguin, 1966), p. 95.

ing. Descartes, as was his wont, thought the ambivalence could be resolved by turning it into a dualism. Our bodies are parts of nature; our minds transcend nature. It is only as composites of mind and body that our position is ambivalent. And if we are careful to keep separate what pertains to mind, to body, and to the intermingling of the two, the way is clear to a form of knowledge which will make us—far from being nature's weakest reeds—its lords and masters.

Descartes's version of self-esteem rests, as we have seen, on understanding ourselves as rational, autonomous wills; and this autonomy is understood in terms of the mind's separation from the realm of nature, which is bound by necessity. It is an ideal of freedom as transcendence of nature. And his sharp distinction between mind and matter reinforces this idea of transcendence. If mind is superior to matter, and there is no longer anything mind-like in the material world, that world becomes inferior to the mind that knows it. With mind now completely withdrawn from matter, its superiority becomes the basis for a new privileged position in relation to the rest of nature. Knowledge was once the understanding of intelligible principles, which were integrated with matter in substantial unities. The knowing intellect was seen as superior to matter but had as its object mind-like forms, which shared that superiority over mere matter. The withdrawal of the forms from matter opens up a conceptual space in which knowledge can be seen as an enactment of the mind's position of dominance, transcending the merely natural. And since the will is central to Descartes's theory of knowledge, this transcendence can be seen as not a simple superiority in status, but an exercise in control. The traditional superiority of form over matter is absorbed into the idea of mind's superiority to produce a new twist to the idea of human dominance. A new vista opens up of a form of knowledge—a "practical philosophy" as Descartes describes it in Part Six of the *Discourse on Method,* through which human beings will become the "lords and masters of nature" (AT vi, 62; Cott. i, 142–43).

Practical and Theoretical Knowledge

Ambivalences have a way of reasserting themselves, undercutting the neat resolutions of dualisms. The enticing clarity of the model of knowledge which comes from the separation of mind from matter becomes more opaque with the intermingling of mind and matter in the Cartesian knower. If human beings are not pure rational wills but rather interminglings of mind with body, it is not clear what position they occupy in nature. What exactly is it of which we are to become masters through knowledge? And what exactly are we who are supposed to reach that goal? The theme of human dominance is complicated by the very sharpness of the mind-body distinction that makes it possible. We are not clear what counts as us and what as nature. Descartes is aware of the problem. In the Sixth Meditation he tries to sort out the shifting uses of the concept of nature which are involved in his theory of mind-body separateness and union. It is a complex but intriguing passage; for here Descartes tries to disentangle not only the different senses of that most shifting of terms—"nature"—but also the shifting relations between human beings and nature, and the way they affect the understanding of knowledge, its scope and rationale.

"Nature," in its most general aspect, Descartes says, means "God himself, or the ordered system of created things established by God" (AT VII, 80; Cott. II, 56). In this sense, his own nature is just the totality of what God has bestowed on him. There is in it no differentiation of good or bad, beneficial or harmful. His talk of nature here evokes a passivity of the mind which seems at odds with the ideal of the domination of nature through knowledge. Nature is cast in the role of teacher, before whom the mind is docile. Nature in this sense is contrasted with what he adds to nature through ill-considered judgment. Nature teaches him that he has a body, that he is closely joined with it—intermingled, so that he and it form a unit. And this brings him to his more restricted sense of nature—what pertains to us as unions, interminglings of mind and body, as distinct from what pertains to mind or body alone. Nature, in this restricted sense, also "teaches." But its deliverances are confined to informing the mind of what is beneficial or harmful for the composite of which it is part. They are misused if taken as reliable touchstones for immediate judgments about the essential nature of the bodies located outside us.

Concern with the well-being of the mind-body composite gives a context for a normative use of the concept of nature. What is natural as part of the totality of being may be, in another sense, unnatural. A sick body is no less a product of the creator than a healthy one. But it may be said to deviate from its nature in craving what will aggravate its disease. It is only with reference to a mind with bodily interests that this concept of the natural can operate. It does not bear on the 'real' natures of things. Things are in this sense natural or unnatural neither with reference to minds nor with reference to bodies alone, but only with reference to the intermingling—to knowers with interests that are bodily. As long as we confine our attention to understanding the nature of a body, its 'deviance' is of no consequence. But when we address the concerns of the mind-body composite, the diseased body, which craves what is bad for it, comes to be seen as a real aberration—a true "error of nature," which must be explained away if we are to preserve the goodness of God. It is from the perspective of the mind-body composite that it seems a travesty. A mind-body composite with a natural craving for what will damage it seems difficult to reconcile with the goodness of God who has bestowed its nature.

As far as the truth of the matter—the truth about matter—is concerned, the dry throat of a healthy human being is no more or less natural than the dry throat of a diseased one. In other words, the distinction between health and disease is extraneous with regard to the understanding of the nature of bodies. But it is quite another matter from the standpoint of the mind-body composite, intent on surviving. Our capacity to crave for what can damage us is no light matter for us as conscious bodily beings, trying to cope with our environment. It makes our own nature appear defective. This distinction between our status as minds, trying to understand matter, and as mind-body composites, trying to persist in that union, grounds for Descartes a distinction between theoretical and practical knowledge. It is only by keeping the two conceptually separate, he thinks, that they can constructively come together in the ideal of a "practical philosophy" that will make us masters of nature.

Descartes has separated the theoretical and the practical in order to bring them together in a new way. It is through increased understanding of the real natures of things, gained through mind alone, that we will become lords and masters of nature. This is knowledge gained through pure intellect, grounded in the rigorous separation of mind from matter, the rejection of the intrusions of sense and imagination. It is quite distinct from the practical knowledge of the beneficial and the harmful, which we arrive at through sensory experience of pleasure and pain. But the pure knowledge of intellect is now given a practical orientation of its own, toward improving the conditions of human life through subduing nature. We understand the natures of things in order to control them, thus extending the province of autonomous will. Descartes's version of freedom, as we have already seen, involves our being able to separate out the things that do depend on our wills from those that do not. But, once we have made that separation, we can, through knowledge, extend the realm of what the will can control. Self-esteem, based on our exemption from the necessities of nature, now passes over into pride in our capacity to dominate the rest of nature for our own purposes.

Descartes's distinctions between mind, body, and their intermingling thus allow him to make the crucial separation between practical and theoretical that underlies his vision of the new era of knowledge. His project involves a withdrawal from nature to reason. Mind retreats from its interminglings with body—the realm of sensory confusion, in which it must negotiate its practical dealings with the world—to the rarified realm of clear and distinct ideas, in which crystalline structures of thought match an equally ordered structure of external reality.[2] But, having carried out that strategic withdrawal, the mind, as rational will, can conduct forays back into the world, extending the realm of its control and hence of its rightful self-esteem. To understand what has happened here it is important to see that the new "practical philosophy" rests, not on Descartes's original practical knowledge, based on pleasures and pains, but on the theoretical knowledge that transcends it. Our transcendence as knowing minds of the intermingling with body grounds relations of transcendence between different forms of knowledge. Spinoza's view of the mind-body relationship opens up the possibility of a very different way of looking at knowledge and its connections with human dominance.

The Domination of Nature

For Spinoza, as we have seen, although we are both minds and bodies, human nature is not an uneasy intermingling of the two. Mind is distinct from body, but not in a way that would allow it to be treated as a separate realm, to which we might repair to plan strategic forays into the buzzing confusion of the world. It is true that he does, especially in his treatment of emotion, distinguish considerations of mind from considerations of body, and of mind and body together. But to think Spinozistically of mind and body together is not to think of an intermingling of two kinds of thing that are in principle separable. It is to think of the same reality in two distinct ways. And, what is more, we cannot think of ourselves as minds without thereby thinking of body. Because the mind is the idea of the body, to think of mind and

2. There are, however, as we saw in Chapter 1, this volume, tensions within Descartes's treatment of sensation. For an interesting discussion of the respects in which Descartes's philosophy takes seriously the role of "bodily based thought" even in theoretical knowledge, see Amélie Rorty, "Descartes on Thinking with the Body," in John Cottingham, ed., *The Cambridge Companion to Descartes* (Cambridge: Cambridge University Press, 1989), pp. 371–92.

body together is just to think body reflectively. We have seen too that he rejects the sharp separation Descartes drew between reflection on our well-being in our dealings with our environment, and theoretical understanding of the natures of things. Clear and distinct thinking remains separable from the confusion of the senses and imagination. But their distinction is not underpinned by a distinction between mind and body as two kinds of reality. The common notions of reason arise from relations of congeniality between ourselves and other things. There is no discontinuity of the kind Descartes draws between scientific knowledge and our reflections on what agrees or disagrees with our nature. Reasoning through common notions does in some ways leave behind that sensory awareness of affinities and dissonances, but not by replacing it with knowledge from a quite different source. The deliverances of reason and the directly felt awareness of body remain on a continuum.

All this means that the possession of reason does not separate human beings out from the rest of nature. Rather, it makes us aware of our integration with it. As the idea of a body that is what it is, and does what it does, only through its insertion into wider totalities, reaching up to the universe as a whole, we are ourselves part of nature, with no privileged position that would allow us to claim exemption from its necessities.[3] We are not, in Spinoza's phrase, located in nature as "a kingdom within a kingdom." We are not, as Descartes thought, its "lords and masters." Despite his rejection of any metaphysically privileged status for human beings in nature, Spinoza's philosophy continues to stress the appropriateness of human domination. His stress on a relation of integration rather than separateness between human beings and the rest of nature does not yield any repudiation of the exploitation of animals. He dismisses such concern as "unmanly" pity. In relation to the animals, we should consider our own advantage, use

3. I discuss the implications of Spinoza's philosophy for environmental ethics in "Spinoza's Environmental Ethics," *Inquiry* 23 (1980), 293–311.

them at our pleasure, and treat them as is most convenient for us (ivP37S1). But this approval of dominance is very differently based from Descartes's. And the view of knowledge that accompanies it is very different from the one founded in Descartes's ideal of control of nature through the autonomous rational will.

Despite the Hegelian view of him as engulfing individuality in the abyss of substance, Spinoza's version of dominance is, like the rest of his philosophy, strongly centered on the recognition of difference. For Descartes the exclusiveness of the human moral community was justified by our possession of a rational soul that transcends body, and hence transcends difference. Animal bodies—and, for that matter, the human body—are automata, although the human body, unlike the bodies of animals, is intermingled with mind. Reason distinguishes us from the beasts. Rather than having less reason than us, he says in the *Discourse on Method,* they have no reason at all (AT vi, 58; Cott. i, 140). In contrast to the autonomy of human agency through the will, it is "nature which acts in them according to the dispositions of their organs" (AT vi, 59; Cott. i, 141). To some extent the same is true of the human body. There is a great deal it can do independently of the mind. Nature acts in it, but the causal power of the human will also acts through it in a way that has no parallel in animal bodies. The automaton that is the human body has capacities that animal automata lack. But the main differences between human and animal bodies are not intrinsic to body but arise rather from the fact that the human body is an instrument of the will.

For Spinoza, in contrast, neither humans nor animals are automata. He does not deny, he says, that the lower animals have sensations (ivP37S1). They have powers and pleasures, but these are different from our own. And it is the differences that justify their exclusion from our moral concerns, our moral community. Nothing can be good except insofar as it agrees with our nature (ivP31C). And what is most useful to us is other human beings, living according to the guidance of reason (ivP35C2). The rational principle of seeking our own advantage demands that human beings join forces with one another, not with the lower animals whose nature and affects do not agree with ours (ivP37S1). "Both the horse and the man are driven by a Lust to procreate; but the one is driven by an equine Lust, the other by a human Lust. So also the Lusts and Appetites of Insects, fish, and birds must vary" (iiiP57S). These distinctive pleasures express, and indeed constitute, the distinctive soul of the individual. It is not lack of feelings that excludes the beasts from the moral considerations appropriate within the human species. What excludes them is the difference between their feelings and ours. We are separated from the beasts by the distinctive character of our emotions, by the affective affinities that bring human beings together. In knowing an individual we know its characteristic joys and pains. Our pains and pleasures define us, and human virtue is nothing but human power—the striving by which we endeavor to persist in being. "So the more each one strives, and is able, to preserve his being, the more he is endowed with virtue" (ivP20Dem).

Different kinds of body involve different kinds of power and virtue. Differences between the powers and pleasures of horses and humans make for differences in soul. And within the human species, differences in pleasure express differences in soul. The pleasures of a drunk are different from those of a philosopher (iiiP57S). (The pleasures of a drunken philosopher, Spinoza does not discuss.) Our individual striving is greatly strengthened by collaboration with others who share our range of affective responses. This is the basis for the exclusion of nonhumans from the moral community. Other species have their own joys, their own lusts. And this means that they cannot collaborate with human beings in a shared pursuit of self-preservation. "Any singular thing whose nature is entirely different from ours can neither aid nor restrain our power of acting, and absolutely no thing can be either good or evil for us, unless it has something in common with us" (ivP29).

So the law against the killing of animals, Spinoza suggests, is "based more on empty superstition and unmanly compassion than sound reason." We have the same right against them as they have against us. Indeed, because the right of each one is defined by his virtue, or power, "men have a far greater right against the lower animals than they have against men" (IVP37S1).

Out of all this there emerges a very different picture of human dominance from the Cartesian one. Our "rights" against other species remain grounded in reason, but not in any privileged position for human beings within nature. The cultivation of human reason, although it has crucial significance for human beings, does not give us any grand metaphysically privileged position. Reason is an expression of human nature, and it arises from the complexity of bodily structure that distinguishes human bodies. It strengthens human powers, especially when pursued in collaboration with other rational beings. But it is circumscribed by human needs, by the demands of human self-preservation. Nature, Spinoza says in the *Theologico-Political Treatise* is not bound by the laws of human nature, which aim only at man's true benefit and preservation. Humanity is "but a speck" in the infinitely wider limits that have reference to "the eternal order of nature."[4] And in the *Ethics,* he stresses that there is no hierarchy of degrees of perfection. We cannot judge the good of other things by reference to ourselves. The perfection of things is to be reckoned only from their own nature and power. A horse is destroyed as much if it is changed into a man as if it is changed into an insect. And perfection in general is just "the essence of each thing insofar as it exists and produces an effect" (IVPref).

Spinoza's ethics is human-centered. But the belief in human superiority on which it rests is different from the Cartesian picture of the transcendence of the mind. On that picture, our minds, being purely intellectual, transcend the limitations of mere unknowing nature,

4. Spinoza, *A Theologico-Political Treatise,* trans. R. H. M. Elwes (New York: Dover, 1951), p. 202.

powerful though its forces may be over our bodies. Cartesian minds rest their self-esteem on that transcendence and the prospects of control which go with it. Spinozistic minds rest their self-esteem on knowing their status as ideas of bodies of a sufficiently complex structure to allow the formation of the common notions of reason. They esteem themselves for the capacity this brings to understand their interdependence with other things and to strengthen their powers by collaboration with the minds of similarly structured bodies. Such minds, like their Cartesian counterparts, would see themselves as superior to other parts of nature. But it is a superiority without transcendence. Collectively we exert a force that can temporarily resist or overcome other natural forces that will ultimately destroy us, mind and body alike. It is a strength that comes from the understanding of interconnections, from the understanding of necessities—not from thinking ourselves exempt from them. We remain part of nature. But that does not mean that we have no right to exert our temporary power over the rest of it. The importance of reason is circumscribed by the needs, desires, and pleasures of a speck in the universe. But its power and importance in relation to that speck are none the less for that.

Spinoza puts human advantage first, just because we, who have an interest in the matter, are human—not because we occupy, from some disinterested standpoint, a privileged position. He refuses to extrapolate from the inevitable human-centeredness of our interests to an anthropocentric view of the world. Things are to be judged with regard to their own well-being and perfection, not ours. His approach takes seriously the sentience and the thriving of other species, and acknowledges that reason itself rests on human "interests," as we might now put the point. Here reason is not at odds with nature, pulling against it and trying to subdue it. Reason is just the mind's power of acting, expressed in the striving for understanding. And the very contrast between conscious reason and unconscious nature, so sharp in the Cartesian view, is blunted here. What makes human beings distinctive is not their possession of a rational soul, utterly different in kind from other parts of nature, but rather the affinities and commonalities that allow them to collaborate with one another and thus strengthen their individual powers.

Sexual Difference

Spinoza's way of stressing the commonalities of human nature avoids the Cartesian abstraction from differences that has become such a strong element in ideals of a human nature, common to all, transcending all merely bodily differences of race or sex. It is interesting to see what happens when we attempt to develop Spinoza's very different way of thinking of sameness and difference in relation to questions of sexual difference—an area that was of course marginal to the concerns of both philosophers.[5] Like Descartes, Spinoza grounds the life of reason in the sameness of human minds. Insofar as human beings are torn by the passions, they disagree in nature, whereas insofar as they live "according to the guidance of reason," they always agree in nature (ivP35). Reason is in all human beings the same. But Spinoza conceptualizes this sameness very differently.

For Descartes, all souls are equally endowed with the capacity for thought, and reason occurs whole and entire in them. All minds must be essentially the same, because they transcend body. And the natural light of reason is supposedly equal in all. The power of judging well and of distinguishing the true from the false, which is properly called "good sense or reason," he says at the beginning of the *Discourse on Method*, is naturally equal in all men. "The diversity of our opinions

5. The ideas in this section draw on my paper "Woman as Other: Sex, Gender, and Subjectivity," *Australian Feminist Studies*, no. 10 (Summer 1989), 13–22. I discuss the "maleness of reason" further in *The Man of Reason: 'Male' and 'Female' in Western Philosophy*, 2d ed. (London: Routledge; and Minneapolis: University of Minnesota Press, 1993) and in "Maleness, Metaphor, and the 'Crisis' of Reason," in Louise Antony and Charlotte Witt, eds., *A Mind of One's Own* (Boulder, Colo.: Westview Press, 1993), pp. 69–84.

does not arise because some of us are more reasonable than others but solely because we direct our thoughts along different paths and do not attend to the same things" (AT vi, 2; Cott. i, iii). By implication, although he does not make it explicit, reason must be naturally equal also in men and women. Sexual difference cannot reach into Cartesian minds. Descartes can nonetheless allow that differences in bodily structure can be associated with differences in intellectual functioning or capacity. Mind's causal transactions with the world must be mediated through different bodies. But those differences are extraneous to the mind; they cannot properly be attributed to the mind itself. So the picture is of minds, which are themselves undifferentiated, intermingling, and causally interacting with, and through, sexually differentiated bodies.

It is a model that lingers in contemporary ideas of sexless minds and sexed bodies intermingling in an uneasy realm of socially constructed 'gender.' For Spinoza, in contrast, since the mind is not a separate intellectual substance but the idea of body, sexual differences can reach right into the mind, although its attribution to bodies still has a certain conceptual priority. Minds could not be sexually differentiated independently of the bodies of which they are ideas. Spinozistic minds, after all, cannot be differentiated at all independently of the bodies of which they are ideas. So difference in mental functioning does not have to be treated, as it is by Descartes, as an effect of an extraneous intermingling with body, from which the true nature of the mind could be extricated. Spinoza's view of the mind-body relationship opens up conceptual space for the possibility that minds are sexually differentiated—a possibility that Descartes's view of the mind closed off. Does this mean that a Spinozistic way of thinking of mind-body relations would commit us to thinking of minds as "male" or "female"? The answer is not straightforward. Why should the idea of a male body be male, we may ask, any more than the idea of a large body is large? This does seem a blatant fallacy from within a Cartesian way of thinking of ideas as modes of an intellectual substance, utterly different in kind from bodies. But there is a way of taking it which is not ludicrous. The idea or mind of a large body is a mind whose nature reflects the "powers and pleasures," in Spinoza's phrase, of a large body. There are distinctive powers and pleasures associated with different kinds of bodily structure. And our minds enact in thought those powers and pleasures. To the extent that the powers and pleasures of human bodies are sexually differentiated, it will then be quite appropriate for a Spinozist to speak of "male" and "female" minds. A female mind will be one whose nature—and "gladness"—reflects its status as idea of a female body. The powers and pleasures of such a body will of course be partly the same as those of a male body. But there will also be differences that cut across other differences and similarities between human bodies.

Because Cartesian minds are simple, transcending all bodily differences, the answer to the question "Are the minds of women the same as those of men?" has to be categorically that they are the same. However complex bodies might be, their differences are transcended in the simplicity of minds. Spinozistic minds, in contrast, reflect the multifacetedness of bodies. They can be alike in some ways, different in others, reflecting the sameness and differences of the bodies of which they are ideas. This suggests that there need not be any specifiable content to what it is to be a "female" or "male" mind. All ideas of female bodies will be, trivially, female. But that does not mean that there is any underlying essence of femaleness which they all have in common. What content they have as minds is determined by the powers and pleasures of the bodies of which they are ideas, and that cannot be known in advance.

This brings us to another important point of contrast between Cartesian and Spinozistic reconstructions of sex and gender. There is for Spinoza continuity between the natural body and the socialized body. The powers of individual bodies are enriched by good forms of social organization which foster the collective pursuit of reason, which enhances human powers and enriches human pleasures. "It is impossible for man not to be a part of nature and not to follow the common order of nature. But if he lives among such individuals as agree with his nature, his power of acting will thereby be aided and encouraged. On the other hand, if he is among such as do not agree at all with his nature, he will hardly be able to accommodate himself to them without greatly changing himself" (ivApp, sect. 7). Among singular things, "we know nothing more excellent than a man who is guided by reason." So we can show best how much our skill and understanding are worth by "educating men so that at last they live according to the command of their own reason" (ivApp, sect. 9).

So much for the men of reason. What of the women? There is little explicit discussion of sexual difference in the *Ethics*. In Part Four, Spinoza makes a passing reference to the Genesis story of Adam and Eve, in which he implies that there is no difference between male and female in respect of rationality. The man, having found a wife who "agreed completely with his nature," knew that there could be nothing in nature more useful to him than she was. But, after he came to believe the lower animals to be like himself, he immediately began to "imitate their affects" and to lose his freedom (ivP68S).

Spinoza's concern here is not with sexual difference but with the relations between freedom and the knowledge of good and evil. His political writings make it clear that, whatever women may be like in the state of nature—if that is how we should describe the location of the Genesis paradise—in the state of society their capacity does not match that of men. They are accordingly excluded from the responsibilities of government.

Sexist though this may appear from our perspective, it is only what we should expect from Spinoza's treatment of reason and nature and his emphasis on the social dimensions of reason. He stresses the interconnections between the life of reason and forms of social organization that enhance freedom. If our natural powers are enriched by the operation of good forms of social organization, which foster the collective pursuit of reason, it is only to be expected that groups excluded from full participation in that shared pursuit of reason will miss out on the full flourishing of their natural powers and pleasures, leading distorted, mutilated lives. If human powers are enriched by the operation of good forms of social organization, it is to be expected that they will be impeded by bad ones, and this state of obstruction is of course the actual position of women, even amidst the good forms of social organization he outlines in the *Theologico-Political Treatise.* Being female in the conditions of that society sets severe restraints on human powers, pleasures, and virtue.

This much of what emerges as a Spinozistic view of sexual difference could be accommodated in a Cartesian framework. The same Cartesian reason must find its way out from the soul into the realm of intermingling with body through more circuitous paths in the case of women. The same mental capacity has a rather more difficult time when intermingled with a female body, and the mind in which it inheres can be expected to achieve rather less in the enterprise of becoming a "lord and master" of nature. But if we take seriously the implications of Spinoza's theory of mind, we must say also that female minds are formed by these socially imposed limitations on the powers and pleasures of female bodies. Differences in male and female experience of the shared social world will mold the minds of women, making them different *as minds* from those that are the ideas of unimpeded male bodies. The bodies of which we are aware, the bodies of which our minds are ideas, have had their powers affected not only by our own "natural" development, but by the social forms that provide a context for that development. Spinozistic bodies are socialized bodies, and our minds reflect that socialization of bodies.

Social arrangements, for better or worse, modify the powers of bodies and, hence, on Spinoza's theory of mind, our awareness of ourselves. There is more to being a male or female body than anatomy. It is a matter of how we move, of posture and gesture, and of the kinds of activity we can perform as socialized bodies. Our minds reflect that socialization. In this way a Spinozistic theory of the mind, in contrast to the Cartesian, can be seen as taking seriously both sex differences and power. Sex differences for Spinoza apply to minds no less than to bodies. But that need not involve the affirmation of any male or female content, existing independently of operations of power.

For Spinoza our minds are not insulated, as they are for Descartes, from the operations of power enshrined in social forms. On this view of the mind, sexual difference is not merely bodily. But this does not mean that there must be some specific content to our awareness of our socialized bodies as male or female. What content this has at any time will reflect the social organization of sex difference—the way collective social power has structured the powers of bodies. But the powers of bodies can in principle always be extricated from the contingent social wholes in which they are embedded, to form new social wholes that may better enhance their powers—as well, of course, as creating ever new possibilities of suppression or oppression. Something remains in all this of the ideal of a shared human nature that transcends difference. But the sameness here, unlike the Cartesian version, is not an already existing metaphysical status, but an ideal of a wholeness to be achieved. Rather than asserting an already existing sameness of soul, underlying the extraneous accretion of bodily differences, the Spinozist ideal aims at achieving commonalities. The participants in such social wholes carry their differences with them. Those differences can be set aside as irrelevant in specific contexts. But they are not minimized, negated, or subsumed under an idealized sameness.

There is of course a biological base for the formation of such social wholes. Bodies have affinities and dissonances, which allow for some forms of social integration and exclude others. Such possibilities and impossibilities, compossibilities and incompatibilities may not be determinable in advance. They are revealed by what bodies can do and are experienced as pleasure or pain, feelings of affinity or disharmony. Sameness of human nature arises from the fact that different bodies have shared affinities that allow their differences to be transcended in the realization of common pleasures. It is a sameness that expresses neither a common higher intellectual nature nor an underlying, circumscribed biological one. Sex differences come out as different ways of experiencing the commonalities of human life, and there is of course more involved in this than the physical differences of male and female bodies. The differences reflect also the influence of social roles and expectations. To pursue Spinoza's example, the physical differences of men and women might not of themselves make all that much difference in the way human beings experience the pleasures of getting drunk or doing philosophy. But the powers and pleasures involved in getting drunk or doing philosophy in seventeenth-century Netherlands society may, for all that, come to something very different for the ideas of male and of female bodies.

Such an approach allows us to say that bodily differences have mental ramifications. Sex differences apply to minds just as much as, and because, they apply to bodies. But, again, this does not mean that we must be able to prescribe any definite content for the differences. To be a male or female mind is to be the idea of a male or female body. Sometimes, in some contexts, being the awareness of a female body will amount to something very different from being the idea of a male body. At other times, and in other contexts, the differences will be minimal. Traits related to sexual difference are changeable, and always, for some minds, the differences will be more important than for others.

The Cartesian way of thinking of minds and bodies—reason transcending mere nature—lingers in contemporary thought of sexless minds and sexed bodies and in an uneasy realm of intermingling, of socially produced gender, which seems unable to engage with either. A Spinozistic way of thinking of sex difference might help resolve some of the impasses that have arisen in contemporary debate about the relations between supposedly biologically given sex and socially constructed gender. Such an approach would take seriously the ramifications of bodily sex differences without affirming any specifiable content for 'true' femininity or masculinity. It could continue to affirm the ideal of a shared human nature, differently sexed though we undoubtedly are, without falling into the Cartesian model of a supposedly already existing sameness of soul. The idea of a shared human nature, on this way of looking at it, would become an ideal of a range of commonalities that can be achieved, not an expression of an already existing sameness.

Such commonalities amidst difference are achievable precisely because our bodies are socialized bodies. The ideal, and the psychic distortions and mutilations it opposes, are made possible by the same fact: that the bodies, of which our minds are ideas, are formed, for better or worse, through the operation of collective human power. This conception of the powers of bodies as modified through social power might open up more fruitful ways of articulating some contemporary feminist aspirations. It could repudiate the spurious 'unsexed soul' that has, with reason, been criticized by some feminists as masking real, socially imposed differences under an idealized sameness. A Spinozistic approach would here take seriously the idea that bodily differences do have ramifications for the minds and selves that we are. But it could do this while avoiding some of the hazards of contemporary feminist affirmations of difference.

Feminist affirmation of difference, in reaction against the idea of gender as transcending sex, and hence malleable almost without limit, has been accompanied by a rejection of the philosophical assumptions implicit in the idea of free-floating gender, especially Descartes's model of the mind-body relationship. The idea of mind as transcending bodily differences has been seen as contributing to a spurious ideal of sameness, to the disadvantage of women. The future is then seen to lie in taking seriously the fact that, as embodied human beings, we are embodied as different sexes. But, in the lack of an alternative way of conceptualizing the relations between mind and body, such affirmations of difference risk 'naturalizing'—and hence rationalizing and perpetuating—some of the content of existing sexual stereotypes.

A Spinozistic approach to these issues allows us both to take seriously the role of the body in our understanding of sex difference and to recognize the contributions of social power to the content of our sexual stereotypes. It allows us to take body seriously, while yet seeing gender as socially constructed all the way through, as it were, rather than as resting on a preexisting and unchangeable base of biological sex difference, in an uneasy causal relationship with gender. It allows us to see our awareness of ourselves as male or female as responding to the experienced facts of bodily sex difference—difference, however, which reflects the operations of social power no less than it reflects biology. On this way of looking at sex difference, there is no sexless soul waiting to be extricated from socially imposed sex roles. But nor is there any authentic male or female identity, existing independently of social power. It allows us to see that, with regard to sexual difference, there are no facts of the matter other than those produced through the shifting play of the powers and pleasures of socialized, embodied, sexed human beings.

O

Conclusion:
Reading Spinoza

Gilles Deleuze refers to Spinoza as belonging to a "counter-history" of philosophy. Like Lucretius, Hume, Nietzsche, and Bergson, he suggests, Spinoza, while seeming to be part of the history of philosophy, seems also to escape it.[1] Such judgments can of course only be made from a historical perspective. They concern the upshot of a philosopher's thought—where it stands in relation to the dominant assumptions of our own ways of thinking, rather than to its own contemporary context. Descartes, revolutionary though his thought was in its own context, is part of our received intellectual framework—a progenitor of our thought patterns—in a way that Spinoza is not. To read Descartes is to read ourselves—to see made explicit some of the basic structures of modern self-consciousness, even if some of them may appear more exotic than they do in the forms in which we now see them. If to read Descartes is to read what we ourselves are, to read Spinoza is to get glimpses of what we might have been—of possibilities of self-consciousness that run against the grain.

It is important not to overstate the presence of Descartes in our own thought patterns. There is of course much else that has contributed to

---

1. Gilles Deleuze and Claire Parnet, *Dialogues,* trans. Hugh Tomlinson and Barbara Habberjam (London: Athlone Press, 1987), pp. 14–15.

our ways of thinking of ourselves. But it cannot be denied that Descartes's thought was subsumed in the development of modern philosophy to become part of the mainstream of modern conscious- ness, shaping the ways we think of ourselves as thinkers and agents, even when the metaphysical machinery that held it together had been discredited. The model of a translucent self, mirroring the structure of an "external" world and hence offering an assured mode of access to knowledge of that world, disintegrated with the receding of the ve- racious God, which held it all together. The pieces fall apart. Without the role of the veracious and beneficent God, all that remains of the Cartesian model is a self-contained substance confronting an irre- trievably external reality. The self-assurance of the Cartesian self depends on God and on its own will, wherein it resembles God. But the God-like will is of little avail in the lack of the God it resembles. A veracious God ensured that both world and self were knowable. The Cartesian self, in the lack of that assurance, becomes an isolated self indeed—alienated, as we have seen, by its very self-completeness. The continuities between self-knowledge and knowledge of the world, which gave such richness to Cartesian self-consciousness, are broken.

But there is another problem too. In the lack of the metaphysical machinery that aligns it with an external world, the Cartesian self does not stay intact. In losing its assured correspondence with a logically ordered reality, it loses also its own inner unity. Within the Cartesian self there lurks the self of fragments often associated with the experi- ence of modernity. We can track the inevitable passage from unity into fragmentation in the subsequent accounts of self-consciousness of- fered by Locke, Berkeley, and Hume.

Like Descartes, Locke uses metaphors of light to describe self- knowledge. But, with his repudiation of innate ideas, the mind be- comes a dark closet, with no windows through which light might enter. There remains a substantial self, underlying ideas, but it is not an object of the mind's direct awareness. The ideas out of which knowledge is constructed come into mind through the senses. They are not revealed through inspection of its own nature. The Lockean self is not a self of fragments. But the removal of self to a deeper level than the ideas of sense breaks the Cartesian nexus between self-knowledge and knowledge of the world. We have a kind of self-knowledge through what Locke calls "ideas of reflection," but these presuppose the ideas of sense. The mind is self-aware through the activities it performs on ideas of sense, not through introspection of its own inner structure. The self's knowledge of itself as substance is attenuated, and mediated through its operations on the ideas of sense which come from outside. Introspective awareness of the flux of perceptions presupposes sensory intake. It is not knowledge of the self as substance. Ideas of sense now become primary and irreducible. They are not transformable, as they were for Descartes, into clear and distinct ideas that comprise the very nature of the self. And, in the lack of Descartes's necessary connections binding clear and distinct ideas together in a unified self, they become discrete mental items, superimposed on an underlying substance that becomes increasingly irrelevant to knowledge. So, although knowledge for Locke still consists in the awareness of 'ideas,' they no longer hold together as a unified self. We do not know intellectual substance in knowing the flow of ideas which makes up our ordinary conscious existence. Locke retains the conviction that the self is a unified intellectual substance, but the self becomes increasingly superfluous to knowledge of the world, and problematic as an object of knowledge at all.

The tensions were already there, as we have seen, in Descartes's picture of the self, especially in his view of the relations between sensation and thought. Descartes sometimes treated sensation as a direct awareness of body, sometimes as a causal process in which the body produces ideas in the mind. With Locke's repudiation of Descartes's treatment of the relations between sensation and thought, the Cartesian conception of the self begins to disintegrate. Locke retains Descartes's treatment of ideas as the proper objects of knowledge, but repudiates his anomalous conception of the relations between sense and pure thought. The immediate objects of the mind's awareness are no longer seen as confused versions of pure thought. Sensory awareness ceases to be a confused intermingling of mind and body. Descartes's equation of self-knowledge with awareness of ideas is left behind and the substantial self, although it remains what knows, becomes increasingly elusive as an object of knowledge.

Berkeley too continued to believe in the existence of the self as a unified intellectual substance, as a 'spirit,' and to equate knowledge with the having of ideas. But self and the ideas that are the objects of knowledge are for him even more polarized than for Locke. Berkeley exploits the implicit superfluousness of matter in the Cartesian system, dispensing with its mediation, so that the physical world results directly from the direct confrontation between 'spirits'—God and the human mind. The relationship between mind and matter is internalized so that it now holds between mind and its "ideas of sensation"—the ideas it finds within itself that, as Descartes himself had pointed out, are not subject to its control. Berkeley's ideas are the "things" of the commonsense world. Matter is shed as superfluous. The self as spirit—far from being a unity of ideas held together through necessary relations—is separated from ideas by the distinction between activity and passivity. Ideas are entirely passive, mind entirely active. Ideas, being passive, can contain no representation of active mind: there can be no idea of the self. Berkeley attempts to retain the possibility of self-knowledge by talking of "notions" of the self. But this marks the opening up of an unbridgeable chasm: if ideas are the objects of knowledge, the self cannot also be an object of knowledge. From Berkeley's difficulties with self-knowledge it is not far to the complete disintegration of the Cartesian model of selfhood in the philosophy of Hume—to the self of fragments, the mere "bundle" of impressions and ideas. The unified single substance becomes a collection of self-contained fragments, each of which, as Hume ironically remarks, could be regarded as satisfying the criteria of substancehood.[2]

Spinoza's treatment of selfhood lies outside this story of the gradual

2. David Hume, *Treatise of Human Nature*, ed. L. A. Selby-Bigge (Oxford: Oxford University Press), Book i, Part IV, sec. V, p. 233.

separation of the substantial self from its ideas, and the self's associated collapse into fragments. Like Hume, he sees the mind as a set of ideas. But he had a basis for the mind's unity which Hume could not provide—both through the necessary connections between ideas and through the mind's status as idea of a body whose unity can be explicated. For him, as we have seen, there is no issue to be resolved about the self's relations to an 'external' world; its direct contact with the rest of the world is written into its nature as idea of body. Nor is there any room for a gap to open between active self and passive ideas, for the mind, like its ideas, is idea of body—liable, like them, to lapse into passivity, but also capable, like them, of transformation into active affirmation. To read Spinoza is thus to glimpse ways of thinking of what it is to be a self in a world which lacks the dilemmas of disintegration and isolation which have afflicted the Cartesian self. It is also to get a clearer idea of just what those dilemmas are. We have seen some of them in the course of this book: the isolation of a self-contained substance trying to reestablish contact with a world beyond itself; the tensions in ideals of personhood which subsume all that differentiates individuals into a supposedly "universal" sameness; the limitations of an ideal of knowledge which demands dichotomies between mind and nature, between the "theoretical" and the "practical," between reason and passions; the discomforts of a way of thinking of time and mortality which allows no middle ground between belief in an afterlife, continuous with individual consciousness, and annihilation.

If Spinoza's treatment of self-consciousness, rather than Descartes's, had been the dominant influence, it would no doubt have given rise to its own dilemmas, its own misfits with modern self-consciousness. We have seen that the Spinozistic self is not vulnerable to the frustrations and disillusionments that afflict a would-be substantial self, when it lacks the theological and metaphysical machinery that held it in secure alignment with its world and assured its own inner unity. But the Spinozistic self has metaphysical dependencies of its own. It does not depend on a transcendent God, but it does rest on the security of being part of a rationally—although not purposefully—ordered, interconnected whole. The security of Spinoza's philosophy is, in its own way, just as inaccessible to us as the idea of the transcendent Cartesian deus ex machina. The point is not that Spinoza's version of rationalism might have succeeded, where Descartes's failed, in providing a stable foundation of self-consciousness to withstand the challenges of modernity. It is rather that reading Spinoza now can open up for us the conceptual space in which we may see the contingency of our received forms of self-consciousness, and the predicaments to which they have given rise. There can be no return to the Spinozistic certainty of our status as parts of a rationally ordered whole. But, like many an outsider, Spinoza, in his very strangeness, can give us increased awareness of what our selfhood is, and of what it might yet be.

Bibliography

Descartes and Spinoza Texts

Adam, Charles, and Paul Tannery, eds. *Oeuvres de Descartes.* Paris: Vrin, 1974–86. 11 vols.

Boyle, Andrew, trans. *Spinoza's "Ethics."* London: Everyman/Dent, 1910.

Cottingham, John, Robert Stoothoff, and Dugald Murdoch, trans. *The Philosophical Writings of Descartes.* 2 vols. Cambridge: Cambridge University Press, 1984–1985.

Curley, Edwin, ed. and trans. *The Collected Works of Spinoza.* Princeton: Princeton University Press, 1985.

Elwes, R. M. H. trans. *The Chief Works of Benedict de Spinoza.* 2 vols. New York: Dover, 1955.

Gebhardt, Carl, ed. *Spinoza Opera.* Heidelberg: Carl Winter, 1925. 4 vols.

Kenny, Anthony, trans. and ed. *Descartes: Philosophical Letters.* Oxford: Clarendon Press, 1970.

Koyré, Alexandre, ed. *Traité de la reforme de l'entendement.* Paris: Vrin, 1974.

Other Works Cited

Allison, Henry. *Benedict de Spinoza: An Introduction.* Rev. ed. New Haven: Yale University Press, 1987.

Antony, Louise, and Charlotte Witt, eds. *A Mind of One's Own: Feminist Essays on Reason and Objectivity.* Boulder, Colo.: Westview Press, 1993.

Aquinas, Thomas. *On the Unity of the Intellect against the Averroists.* Trans. Beatrice H. Zedler. Milwaukee: Marquette University Press, 1968.

Bibliography

Bayle, Pierre. *Ecrits sur Spinoza.* Textes choisis et présentés par Françoise Charles-Daubert et Pierre-François Moreau. Paris: Berg International Editeurs, 1983.

Bennett, Jonathan. *A Study of Spinoza's "Ethics."* Cambridge: Cambridge University Press, 1984.

Cottingham, John, ed. *The Cambridge Companion to Descartes.* Cambridge: Cambridge University Press, 1989.

Curley, Edwin. *Behind the Geometrical Method: A Reading of Spinoza's "Ethics."* Princeton: Princeton University Press, 1988.

———. *Spinoza's Metaphysics: An Essay in Interpretation.* Cambridge: Harvard University Press, 1969.

Curley, Edwin, and Pierre-François Moreau, eds. *Spinoza: Issues and Directions.* Leiden: Brill, 1990.

Delahunty, R. J. *Spinoza.* London: Routledge and Kegan Paul, 1985.

Deleuze, Gilles. "Spinoza et nous." *Actes du Colloque International Spinoza.* Paris, 3–5 May 1977. Paris: Albrui Michel, 1978.

———. *Spinoza: Philosophie pratique.* Paris: Albrui Michel, 1978. Trans. Robert Hurley as *Spinoza: Practical Philosophy.* San Francisco: City Lights Books, 1988.

Deleuze, Gilles, and Claire Parnet. *Dialogues.* Trans. Hugh Tomlinson and Barbara Habberjam. London: Athlone Press, 1987.

Donagan, Alan. *Spinoza.* Chicago: University of Chicago Press, 1989.

———. "Spinoza's Proof of Immortality." In Marjorie Grene, ed. *Spinoza: A Collection of Critical Essays,* pp. 241–48. New York: Anchor Press/Doubleday, 1973.

Gadamer, Hans-Georg. "Hegel's Dialectic of Self-Consciousness." In *Hegel's Dialectic: Five Hermeneutical Studies,* trans. P. Christopher Smith. New Haven: Yale University Press, 1976, pp. 54–74.

Grene, Marjorie. *Descartes.* Minneapolis: University of Minnesota Press, 1985.

———. *Spinoza: A Collection of Critical Essays.* New York: Anchor Press/Doubleday, 1973.

Grene, Marjorie, and Debra Nails, eds. *Spinoza and the Sciences.* Boston Studies in the Philosophy of Science, vol. 91. Dordrecht: Reidel, 1986.

Hampshire, Stuart. *Spinoza.* Harmondsworth, U.K.: Penguin, 1987.

Hegel, Georg Wilhelm Friedrich. *Lectures on the History of Philosophy.* 1896, Vol. 3. Trans. Elizabeth S. Haldane and Frances H. Simson. London: Routledge and Kegan Paul; New York: Humanities Press, 1974.

Bibliography

———. *Phenomenology of Spirit.* Trans. A. V. Miller. Oxford: Oxford University Press, 1977.

———. *Shorter Logic.* Trans. William Wallace. Oxford: Oxford University Press, 1904.

Hume, David. *Treatise of Human Nature.* 1734–46. Ed. L. A. Selby-Bigge. Oxford: Oxford University Press.

Kashap, S. Paul, ed. *Studies in Spinoza.* Berkeley: University of California Press, 1972.

Kennington, Richard, ed. *The Philosophy of Baruch Spinoza.* Studies in Philosophy and the History of Philosophy, vol. 7. Washington, D.C.: Catholic University of America Press, 1980.

Kneale, Martha. "Eternity and Sempiternity." *Proceedings of the Aristotelian Society,* vol. 69, pp. 223–38. Reprinted in Marjorie Grene, ed., *Spinoza: A Collection of Critical Essays,* pp. 227–40.

Leibniz, Gottfried Wilhelm. *Philosophical Papers and Letters.* Trans. Leroy E. Loemker, 2d ed. Dordrecht: Reidel, 1969.

Lloyd, Genevieve. "Maleness, Metaphor, and the 'Crisis' of Reason." In Louise Antony and Charlotte Witt, eds., *A Mind of One's Own.* Boulder: Westview Press, 1993, pp. 69–84.

———. *The Man of Reason: 'Male' and 'Female' in Western Philosophy.* 2d ed. London: Routledge, and Minneapolis: University of Minnesota Press, 1993.

———. "Spinoza on the Distinction between Intellect and Will." In Edwin Curley and Pierre-François Moreau, eds., *Spinoza: Issues and Directions,* pp. 113–24. Leiden: Brill, 1990.

———. "Spinoza's Environmental Ethics." *Inquiry* 23 (1980), 293–311.

———. "Spinoza's Version of the Eternity of the Mind." In Marjorie Grene and Debra Nails, eds., *Spinoza and the Sciences,* pp. 211–33. Boston Studies in the Philosophy of Science, vol. 91. Dordrecht: Reidel, 1986.

———. "Woman as Other: Sex, Gender, and Subjectivity." *Australian Feminist Studies,* no. 10 (Summer, 1989), 13–22.

Macherey, Pierre. *Hegel ou Spinoza.* Paris: François Maspéro, 1979.

Maimonides, Moses. *The Guide for the Perplexed.* Trans. M. Friedlander. New York: Dover, 1956.

Mark, Thomas. *Spinoza's Theory of Truth.* New York: Columbia University Press, 1972.

———. "Truth and Adequacy in Spinozistic Ideas." In Robert W. Shahan and John I. Biro, eds., *Spinoza: New Perspectives,* pp. 11–34. Norman: University of Oklahoma Press, 1978.

Bibliography

Pascal, Blaise. *Thoughts.* Trans. Alban J. Krailsheimer. Harmondsworth, U.K.: Penguin, 1966.

Rorty, Amélie. "Descartes on Thinking with the Body." In John Cottingham, ed., *The Cambridge Companion to Descartes,* pp. 371–92. Cambridge: Cambridge University Press, 1989.

——. "Spinoza on the Pathos of Idolatrous Love and the Hilarity of True Love." In Robert C. Solomon and Kathleen M. Higgins, eds., *The Philosophy of (Erotic) Love,* pp. 352–71. Lawrence: University Press of Kansas, 1991.

Santayana, George. Introduction to Spinoza's *Ethics.* Trans. A. Boyle. London: Everyman/Dent, 1910.

Sartre, Jean-Paul. *Being and Nothingness.* Trans. Hazel E. Barnes. New York: Philosophical Library, 1956.

Scruton, Roger. *Spinoza.* Oxford: Oxford University Press, 1986.

Sprigge, Timothy. "Ideal Immortality." *Southern Journal of Philosophy* vol. 10, (Summer 1972), 219–36.

Taylor, Alfred E. "Some Incoherencies in Spinozism, Part II." *Mind* 46, 281–301. Reprinted in S. Paul Kashap, ed., *Studies in Spinoza.* Berkeley: University of California Press, 1972.

Tolstoy, Leo. *"The Death of Ivan Ilyich" and Other Stories.* Trans. Rosemary Edmonds. London: Penguin, 1960.

Wilson, Margaret Dauler. *Descartes: Ego Cogito Ergo Sum.* London: Routledge and Kegan Paul, 1978.

——. "Objects, Ideas and 'Minds': Comments on Spinoza's Theory of Mind." In Richard Kennington, ed., *The Philosophy of Baruch Spinoza:* Studies in Philosophy and the History of Philosophy, vol. 7, pp. 103–20. Washington, D.C.: Catholic University of America Press, 1980.

Wittgenstein, Ludwig. *Tractatus Logico-Philosophicus.* 1918. Trans. David F. Pears and Brian F. McGuiness. London: Routledge and Kegan Paul; New York: Humanities Press, 1961.

Wolfson, Harry A. *The Philosophy of Spinoza* 1934; New York: Meridian, 1958.

Yovel, Yirmiyahu. *Spinoza and Other Heretics.* 2 vols. Princeton: Princeton University Press, 1989.

O

Index

Index

Intellect, 32, 37, 40, 56, 59–75; and will, 59–75
Interconnection, 10–11, 20, 29, 159, 163, 171
Introspection, 3, 171
Intuition, 105–7, 110, 114, 129–30, 138–41, 144
Irony, 9, 78, 104

Joy, 74, 84–98, 102–3, 106, 119–20, 157
Judgment, 48–49, 59–75, 83, 151

Kant, Immanuel, 63, 103, 145
Knowledge: and dominance, 147, 149–50, 156; of good and evil, 80–97, 163; kinds of, 109, 114, 139, 141; practical and theoretical, 105, 151–59
Koyré, Alexandre, 55

Leibniz, Gottfried Wilhelm, 13, 64, 68, 71, 73, 119
Life, 116, 132, 137, 141–45
Light, 6, 59, 108, 170
Locke, John, 170
Love, 29–30, 74–75, 81, 87–93, 125. *See also* God: intellectual love of

Macherey, Pierre, 7
Maimonides, 125, 127
Male. *See* Sexual difference
Mark, Thomas, 53, 54
Mathematics, 37, 77, 110
Memory, 133–34
Metaphors, 6, 48, 71, 108, 170
Mind-body relation, 16–25, 33, 36–38, 57, 84, 88, 90–93, 105, 123–29, 150–54, 161, 166, 172
Moral community, 156–57
Motion, 11, 13–14, 17, 28

Necessary connections, 171–73
Necessity, 51, 60, 100, 104, 111, 114, 150, 155, 159

Obsession, 29–30
Oldenburg, Henry, 12

Pain, 29, 78, 105, 165
Parnet, Claire, 169
Particulars, 141–42
Pascal, Blaise, 149
Passions, 29, 60, 77–104, 109, 128
Passivity, 47, 64, 85, 93–104, 172
Past, 106, 129, 137–38
Perfection, 158–59
Perspectives, 12, 21–25, 43, 49–50, 55, 130, 141
Pineal gland, 80, 84
Pity, 81, 155
Pleasure, 29, 78, 84, 105–6, 157, 162–68
Power, 101–2, 106, 157–58, 162–68
Present, 88, 106, 116, 137–38
Propositions, 22, 25–26
Providence, 65–67

Rationalism, 1–2, 43, 174
Reason: and body, 155–68; limitations of, 52–53, 107–10, 138–41; and passions, 60, 77–104, 106; and senses, 33, 43–45. *See also* Common notions
Reflection, 20, 55–56, 105, 171
Rights, 157–60
Romanticism, 1–3
Rorty, Amélie, 29, 154
Rousseau, Jean Jacques, 1

Sadness, 81, 85–97, 102–3
Santayana, George, 137–38
Sartre, Jean-Paul, 24
Science, 3, 60, 78, 105

Index